Latinos in the End Zone

DOI: 10.1057/9781137403094

Latino Pop Culture

Series Editor: **Frederick Luis Aldama**

Books in the series give serious critical attention to all facets of Latino popular culture. Books focus on topics generally that pertain to the making and consuming of Latino pop culture, including music, performance and body art, TV shows, film, comic books, web media, pop art, low-riders, sartorial wear, video games, sports, and cuisine, among many other areas.

Titles include:

Frederick Luis Aldama and Christopher González
LATINOS IN THE END ZONE
Conversations on the Brown Color Line in the NFL

DOI: 10.1057/9781137403094

palgrave▸pivot

Latinos in the End Zone: Conversations on the Brown Color Line in the NFL

Frederick Luis Aldama

Arts and Humanities Distinguished Professor of English,
Ohio State University, USA

and

Christopher González

Texas A&M University-Commerce, USA

DOI: 10.1057/9781137403094

First published in 2014 by
PALGRAVE MACMILLAN®
in the United States—a division of St. Martin's Press LLC,
175 Fifth Avenue, New York, NY 10010.

Where this book is distributed in the UK, Europe and the rest of the world,
this is by Palgrave Macmillan, a division of Macmillan Publishers Limited,
registered in England, company number 785998, of Houndmills,
Basingstoke, Hampshire RG21 6XS.

Palgrave Macmillan is the global academic imprint of the above companies
and has companies and representatives throughout the world.

Palgrave® and Macmillan® are registered trademarks in the United States,
the United Kingdom, Europe and other countries.

ISBN: 978-1-137-40310-0 EPUB
ISBN: 978-1-137-40309-4 PDF
ISBN: 978-1-137-40308-7 Hardback

Library of Congress Cataloging-in-Publication Data is available from the
Library of Congress.

A catalogue record of the book is available from the British Library.

First edition: 2014

www.palgrave.com/pivot

DOI: 10.1057/9781137403094

*For our girls Corina, Olivia, and Emilia—
the next gen of Latina/o athletes*

DOI: 10.1057/9781137403094

Contents

DOI: 10.1057/9781137403094

Preface: A Life Unexamined Is Not Worth Living

Our book sets out to uncover the invisible history of Latino professional football players in the National Football League, or NFL. In recent years, the NFL has been a professional league where Latinos have seemingly thrived in the high-profile positions of many of the marquee franchises. Yet the nearly century-old history of the NFL reveals that Latino players are not a new feature to the most popular professional sports league in the U.S. The sudden rise of Latino players exposes a lacuna in the NFL's history. It makes us ask where the Latino football players have been all this time.

While there have been many significant examinations of the intersections of Latinidad and American sports culture, there have been no book-length studies that exclusively excavate the Latino history of the NFL. In *Latinos in the End Zone* we trace the development of professional football as it coincides with the inclusion and participation of Latinos within the game. In order to allow for a free-flowing yet far-reaching exploration of our topic, we envisioned a Socratic dialogue where a great many related topics might be broached in an economy of space. Though we are both scholars accustomed to publishing in many different formats, choosing to give this history the shape of a conversation allowed us to maintain our separate voices (and with these our differing experiences and knowledge). This made for a judicious contrapuntal interplay of two independent voices that move in and around one another to create the total composition that tells the cultural, historical, sociopolitical story of Latinos in the NFL.

Our ensemble of contrapuntal voices come together in the careful orchestration of exposition (Prologue), development (its interior five major chapters), and crescendo (Epilogue). The middle sections are composed as follows: Chapter 1, "From Scrimmage Lines to End Zones: Latinos in the National Football League," provides a nuanced socio-cultural analysis of exclusionary practices and trends in the early history of the pro leagues. Chapter 2, "From Punishing Penalties to Brown Bodies *Raiding* the NFL," considers several significant moments when Latinos *broke* through the brown color line, including the pivotal moment when two of the NFL's most significant Latino figures Tom Flores (coach) and Jim Plunkett (quarterback) took the Oakland Raiders to two Super Bowl victories. Chapter 3, "Sidelined...*No Más!*", considers issues of access to education (GI Bill, athletic scholarships, and Affirmative Action), the increased regional diversification and heritage of Latino players (from urban to rural regions and of Mexican, Puerto Rican, Dominican, and Cuban origin), and the presence of Latinos in the globalization of the game. Chapter 4, "The Blitz...Heroes, Saviors, Saints, and Sinners," considers the role of the community, the media, and capitalism generally in the rise and fall of Latino superstar players. Chapter 5, "Three Latino Legends: Snapshot by Interview," includes conversations we conducted with three Latino football pioneers: Joe Kapp, Tom Flores, and Jim Plunkett. We turn to our elders to learn from their wealth of experience and wisdom as significant shapers in the history of the NFL.

With *Latinos in the End Zone*, we make the case that Latinos have a great stake in the game of professional football, both on the field as participants and as spectators who help drive the economic engine of the NFL. This is a history built out of collective voices and experiences. In many ways it is the weaving together of oral histories to convey the collective and collaborative work of those Latinos that made this history. What better way to tell this story than as a conversation—a dramatic narrative that includes more than us but that reaches out to you as the reader to participate in this exploratory journey of life in its myriad forms and activities.

DOI: 10.1057/9781137403094

Prologue: Kick Offs

Abstract: *Prologue, "Kick Offs," establishes the parameters for Frederick Luis Aldama and Christopher González's conversación de sobremesa—a tradition in Latino culture of discussing subjects in great detail and at great length after dinner. They begin by juxtaposing their own autobiographical experience with lucid cultural analysis of Latinos in pro football leagues—and not fútbol as in soccer. They offer a hermeneutical approach that seeks to assign meaning to the material and intellectual culture of Latinos in the NFL; they establish their approach to assess and assert the value and importance of the struggles and victories experienced by the significant yet oft-overlooked presence of Latinos in the history of pro football.*

Frederick Luis Aldama and Christopher González. *Latinos in the End Zone: Conversations on the Brown Color Line in the NFL.* New York: Palgrave Macmillan, 2014. DOI: 10.1057/9781137403094.

Frederick Luis Aldama: Before we launch into this much needed conversation on Latinos in the National Football League I have a confession to make:

Unlike you, Christopher, I don't have any semblance of a sublime football spiral anywhere in my past; I don't have a football bone in my body. There were plenty of Latino kids in my neighborhood in Sacramento that did like to toss an oblong shaped ball around more than kick a black & white checkered round ball, but I wasn't one of them. I certainly relished in the spectacle of it all and enjoyed my "Breakfast of Champions" Wheaties to get me going in the morning, but that's about as close as I came to the sport....

Christopher González: I come from a family that values sport seemingly *in extremis*—almost to the point where being an athlete was the expression, pride, and culmination of the family's gene pool. My brothers and uncles excelled in athletics, and I was expected to follow suit, especially because the men in my family are all large. (I'm one of the smaller men in my immediate family at 6'2", 235 lbs.) I can remember being in the sixth grade, showing interest in enrolling in band because I really wanted to play an instrument. My mother would have none of it, and she let me know quite clearly. Later in high school I discovered that I had the talent to throw the shot put and discus at an elite level (it ultimately funded my undergraduate degree), and so playing football fell by the wayside relatively quickly for me because I wanted to devote all of my training to improving as a track and field athlete. But my interest and passion in football have never flagged, and as long as I can remember I've paid close attention to the NFL.

FLA: My interest from the sidelines as a kid has grown into a more formal, interpretive, interest in football today. It has grown into a scholarly watchfulness that attends especially to football *and* Latinos. My ears perk up when I hear about a Latino in the NFL...or having joined my university's team, The Buckeyes. I become sharp-eyed and laser focused when anything to do with Latinos in football run ticker-tape across media screens...

CG: That makes sense, especially because we're talking about football. That is to say, *American* football and not *fútbol* (soccer). Watch any MLB game and you'll see so many Latinos that it has become normalized. No one thinks twice about seeing a Rivera, a Cabrera, a Rodriguez, and so on play in the big leagues of America's pastime. But to see Latinos playing

DOI: 10.1057/9781137403094

football seems like an exceptional circumstance even today. It is starting to change, and that's why I think a book like this is such an important thing to write. Not only have we initiated a conversation here, but we've hopefully begun a larger discussion about Latinos and football as well.

FLA: Christopher, we can take several tacks in our approach to Latinos in the NFL: social, economic, cultural, historical, for instance. All are valid. As I think we'll see as our book-length conversation—shall we consider it a *conversación de sobremesa?*—unfolds, we will have to touch on all of these, and more...

CG: I think it's the only way to take on this intriguing topic because all of the tacks you mention are interconnected. It's hard to make each one into a discrete issue for examination. Having our exploration unfold as a personable dialogue—a *conversación de sobremesa*—as you aptly put it, will actually allow us to emphasize these and other issues in a fluid manner rather than a rigid structure that might preclude some of the necessary nuance to our discussion.

FLA: An important part of our work as scholars is as interpreters of culture. Of course, this can be done and *is* done by people without any academic training. It's done by people all the time—and not just in blogs, but also in all their activities. Interpretation is as much a part of human activity as the making of culture.

However, we've decided to focus our attention on a particular product of human activity—the cultural phenomenon of Latinos in football—in as rigorous and at the same time interpretive capacity as possible. In a hermeneutical effort we seek to assign meaning to the material and intellectual culture of Latinos in the NFL to assess and assert its value and importance in the world...

CG: Indeed, one of the more common types of commentary in sports, and particularly in the NFL, is the former player as analyst. Of course having these insider experts who share insights gained from experience within the game itself adds value to the sport. Politics has its pundits; the NFL has its commentators. They perform the very important work of explaining to fans what happens on the field and inside the locker room.

On the other hand, because the NFL is such a dominant aspect of the American culture, what happens with the NFL (both on and off the field) necessitates interpreters of culture as well. In other words, the NFL plays such a significant role in American culture that everyone—from your co-workers to late-night talk show hosts—is going to take a stab at making sense of it all. We bring our own skill set to understanding how Latinos and Latino culture are shaped by the NFL, and vice versa—a very *necessary* thing, in my estimation. If you and I—scholars of Latino cultural phenomena—don't take up these issues, we do a disservice by waiting for someone else to bring up the topic, if they do at all.

FLA: As our *conversación de sobremesa* unfolds I think we'll find that we will have to touch on sweepingly broad topics (all that relates to life within a social tissue built out of the socioeconomics of capitalism) as well as those that pertain more to the Latino way of life at the level of family and community: from experiences of race, gender, and sexuality prejudices to eating and physical activities to myth making and breaking as well as hero worship and hero sacrifice....

CG: I'm already anticipating how we will go about exploring our over-arching topic, and it strikes me that we'll have to lay down some brief but necessary exposition in order to allow these topics to resonate as they should. When you say "the socioeconomics of capitalism," one couldn't find a better exemplar than the NFL. It is the pinnacle of human performance as translated into revenue, arguably unlike any other sport on the planet. Millions of dollars are made and lost on the difference of two-tenths of one second at the NFL combine every year. And considerations of the other important issues you mention will be pillars of our conversation, I'm sure.

FLA: As we both know well, brown bodies have populated the territories that make up the Southwestern region of the U.S. long before people identified as of the United States of America. However, because of all sorts of social and economic policies of discrimination that began with gatekeeping access to education, Latinos had been historically kept out of amateur and professional sports...

CG: You raise the important issue of education, Frederick, and I'm glad that we can talk about it early in our *conversación*. Despite the stereotypical distinction between being a scholar and a jock, it's worth noting that, except in extraordinary circumstances, you cannot gain entry into either amateur or professional sports without gaining entry into institutions of higher learning. In the Super Bowl era of the NFL (1970–present), you'll not find any players who were drafted without having first been recruited by a collegiate football program. The MLB

DOI: 10.1057/9781137403094

and NBA are exceptions to this, as they often recruit players directly from high school. But since our focus is on the NFL, it is safe to say that if a player isn't accepted into an institution of higher learning, he'll not be playing in the NFL. Colleges and universities function exactly as gatekeepers for the NFL, and the current policy is that any player who is draft eligible must be out of high school for a minimum of three years. And while there is not a codified rule that players must be in college, it's standard operating procedure that the NFL will not consider a player who hasn't played collegiate football. It's one of the most important ways they gauge prospective talent—by studying how a prospect played in college.

Now, if we think of access to education as a significant barrier with which Latinos have historically had to contend, then we may as well say that the same barrier served as a barrier of entrance into the NFL. Admittance into a collegiate program is crucial for the development of the future NFL player—from facilities, to coaching, to financial resources such as scholarships, and so forth. And even those Latinos who are admitted into collegiate programs often have the struggle of affording college. What I mean here is that the Latino family structure tends to have an "all hands on deck" approach when dealing with matters of money. Working family members contribute—in part or in full— financial earnings for the good of the family. Now, if a young Latino male goes off to university, the family is deprived of a potential earner. In turn, the Latino male student may not have the sort of financial resources from family as other students might. What I'm outlining is not definitive in all instances; there are exceptions. However, my point is to note that not only has it been difficult for Latino students to gain fair entry into universities, the economics of such an opportunity often create barriers in their own right.

FLA: In the mid-2000s I first began seriously attending to the presence (or lack thereof) of Latinos in the NFL. At this time, I not only noticed a curious absence in scholarship on the subject but also, as I sifted through the stats for 2006, that there had only been 19 Latino players out of approximately the 1,700 who played that year. After a little more scratching, I confirmed what I'd known intuitively: Latinos were playing football in the streets as kids and even at school with organized sports but they were not making it through the pipeline. At that time I counted only a hundred or so Latino football players in the entire history of the pro football game...

DOI: 10.1057/9781137403094

CG: You mention that you knew this intuitively; so did I. And still, I find those numbers staggering. And your description of a pipeline is a spot-on metaphor. One has to get *to* the pipeline if he has a chance at making it *through* the pipeline. The pipeline begins in high school, though some universities are recruiting and offering scholarships to star football players even as young as eighth graders, as Alabama and LSU did in the spring of 2013. But what does it take to get through the pipeline, beyond the obvious issue of elite talent and ability? This is where education and the family come to the fore. There is a cultural disconnect between the Latino family, the education system, and the capitalist football enterprise. (No other sport generates revenue for high schools and universities like football.) I believe it is a combination of socioeconomic factors and prejudicial policies that have created this vacuum of Latinos in the NFL.

FLA: How far do we travel back in time to sleuth out the root of the problem? It's a fact that since the signing of the Treaty of Guadalupe Hidalgo in 1848 Latinos have been treated as second and third class citizens in the U.S. It's a fact that Latinos faced Jim Crow-like policies of segregation in education through the first half of the 20th century. It's a fact that Latino children were given serious set backs within a segregated public school system that underfunded, understaffed and with under educated teachers, and under resourced schools attended by Latinos. With punitive prohibitions against Spanish monolingual and Spanish/English bilingual speakers, schools served as labs for assimilation and vocational training.

CG: This is what we are identifying as the "brown color line" in the subtitle of our book.

FLA: It's this brown color line that played out in the lives of Latinos who sought to become football players, but were never able to realize this ambition. As we know from our conversations with Latino pioneers of the game, this also played a central role in the struggles of those like Joe Kapp and Tom Flores and many other early players of the game. We see clearly from their lives that this brown color line was created by unequal access to education and racial segregation just mentioned; can you believe that there were regions in the U.S. that forbid Latinos from using public swimming pools on certain days of the week? One way or another, the Latino football players hit this brown color line—a line expressed through a deep prejudice and that has continued to create a disparity between life for Latinos in the U.S. and those of Anglos.

DOI: 10.1057/9781137403094

CG: It's that whole thing of feeling like a foreigner in your own land. For decades Latinos would find the American education system an inhospitable place. I recall a story my mother told me time and again when I was a child. It's a story familiar to many Spanish-speaking Latinos who grew up in the 1960s and 1970s. A boy in her third-grade class couldn't speak English, and so my mother, being bilingual, translated the teacher's instructions to the boy. My mother wound up in trouble for speaking Spanish (strictly forbidden), and she received corporal punishment for it from the principal. Her father, my grandfather, made it very clear, in no uncertain terms, that the principal had better think twice before he ever laid a finger on my mother. As I've suggested, my mother's story is not unique, yet it serves to illustrate just how unwelcoming an environment a school could be to a Latino or Latina child. For much of the 20th century, Latino students merely wanted to survive school. And often, because it was such an antagonistic environment, many Latino students just wanted to get out of the education system as swiftly as possible, even if it meant dropping out before graduation.

FLA: In the 1920s, so-called intelligence testing of Latinos went hand in hand with physical ability testing. In both, Latinos were deemed intellectually fit only for physical labor and biologically unfit for playing sports. Latinos were considered too lazy, undisciplined, and intellectually inferior to play sports....

CG: Only recently, and through great pains, have these sorts of tests become somewhat valid. Culturally ignorant exams and measures often equated a lack of cultural knowledge with lower intelligence. The same occurred with physical ability testing. For example, consider a Latino child who delights in playing soccer and may never have had an opportunity to develop the skill set to play basketball. A test designed to measure the ability to dribble a basketball isn't a fair measure of this particular kid's physical ability. One can readily imagine other scenarios where physical ability tests were created and conducted without a proper understanding of specific cultural norms. Also, stereotypes persist when specific knowledge and experience are unavailable. Teachers and coaches who may have already held cultural biases, perhaps even without realizing it, predisposed Latino students as being incapable of success in specific areas of sport.

FLA: Grown in such educational conditions heavy with ideological indoctrination and emaciated in material and intellectual resources it's

DOI: 10.1057/9781137403094

not too much of a surprise that we only see a few sprinkles of Latinos in amateur and professional sports in the first half of the 20th century...

CG: As a rule, the odds of becoming a successful amateur or professional athlete are nearly infinitesimal. I remember as an undergraduate college athlete being told that the chances of earning a living as an athlete should not have been a feasible goal for most NCAA athletes. Thus, we (the college athletes) needed to prepare for a professional life outside of our athletic field. In short, even if you have the drive, the resources, the willpower, and opportunity on your side, *you still will most likely not become a career athlete!* Consider, then, how much more difficult it is for those who have certain barriers to surmount that other athletes don't have to negotiate in their own climb for athletic success. Whether it is the result of an education system that has not been supportive and proactive for Latino students for much of its history, or the suspicion or devaluation with which Latino families view the American education system, or, as I suspect, a combination of these, large swaths of Latinos didn't have access and facilitation through the pipeline as other groups might have.

FLA: We do begin to see a few Latinos in the 1930s and 1940s appear in the pro American Football League and the Canadian league. We know that this was not the result of huge civil rights gains. I wonder, as seen with Native American athletes like Jim Thorpe, if this wasn't a consequence of this epoch's use of sports in schools across the country to assimilate non-whites.

CG: You bring up two issues here, and I'd like to tease out both of them. I'll begin with Jim Thorpe then come back to the appearance of Latinos in the 1930s and 1940s in sports.

We live in an age where the use of performance enhancing drugs (PEDs) is ubiquitous if not expected. As I write this, Ryan Braun, major league baseball star of the Milwaukee Brewers, has been suspended for the remainder of the season without pay for violating the MLB's drug policy. Mind you, Braun was the NL's MVP for 2011. And his suspension comes on the heels of the Lance Armstrong revelations in 2012. Suffice it to say that, because we understand that PEDs are always a few steps ahead of tests designed to detect them, we now view sports through the lens of the so-called steroid era. Unlike the American legal system that bestows upon individuals the presumption of innocence, great athletes today are suspected of cheating until a test confirms our suspicion.

DOI: 10.1057/9781137403094

But Jim Thorpe was the type of athlete that would have been one of the elite talents even in the steroid era, such was his preternatural physical prowess. Today we are in a time of specialized athletes who focus all their training and energy toward one sport or event. To divert time and dedication to more than one athletic pursuit is seen as wasteful. But Thorpe was the best in nearly every sporting event he pursued. It would be like taking today's best football player, the world's best Olympic decathlete, and MLB's best baseball player and rolling them into one. Now throw in basketball and lacrosse. It's simply unheard of but for Thorpe. And to make matters more interesting, Thorpe was a Native American of the Sac and Fox tribe. He lived in a time of widespread injustices of inequality, and for that reason he is a sort of progenitor of Jesse Owens and Jackie Robinson in that their physical talents superseded institutional racial barriers. Might Thorpe still have garnered his sports accolades if he had gone by his indigenous name, Wa-Tho-Huk? We'll never know.

Yet consider how many other players belonging to minority groups we can list from Thorpe's era. They are few and far between, and that's being kind. Thorpe was so recognized for his uncanny athleticism that many sports organizations have claimed him as one of their own. Just last year I visited the Pro Football Hall of Fame in Canton, OH, and the first exhibit you encounter is dedicated to Thorpe. You literally cannot see the rest of the exhibits without paying homage to the dynamic bronze statue of Thorpe in midstride, cradling a football before him in his right arm. A later exhibit of Thorpe states: "Jim Thorpe: This fabled athlete gave pro football its first 'big name' when he joined the 1915 Canton Bulldogs. Many insist he was the greatest football player who ever lived and the National Football League had a special spot for Jim Thorpe on its all-time all-star team. He was called simply: 'THE LEGEND.'" The NFL essentially founds its organization on the talent of a player of Native American descent, and yet to this day sees nothing problematic with having one of its teams dubbed as "Redskins." It speaks to how tone deaf the organization is on issues of race and identity, primarily because it is a business that makes vast sums of profit above all else.

In terms of how sports were used in schools during the early 20th century, there were clear intentions to use them as a means of assimilation. However, that didn't readily translate to assimilation in post-high school sports. I mentioned Jackie Robinson a moment ago, and he stands as the epitome of an athlete that was able to break through the barrier of segregated sports. One thinks of the Native American baseball leagues

DOI: 10.1057/9781137403094

that date back as far, and some even farther, than so-called American baseball leagues. LeAnne Howe has done terrific work in this area, and her book *Miko Kings* highlights the importance of Native American baseball leagues. Her book also emphasizes how many great Native American baseball players were kept out of white leagues, and as a result, how these men's stats were erased because they weren't "sanctioned" or "official." So, despite the fact that minority youths could engage in sports at a primary or secondary school level, they would never be allowed to enter the mainstream sports arena *unless* they happened to be, quite literally, the world's greatest athlete like Thorpe.

FLA: It could also just as well be that more Latinos were finding the back door into the sport. That one Latino kid with exceptional athletic talent who tossed the football with his pals in the streets and parks who is recognized by that one open-minded coach and encouraged (and even trained) to run with the ball all the way through to the end zones of the pro leagues.

CG: True, though we have to remember how rare it would have been to find an open-minded coach in the early to mid-20th century. That's not to say there weren't any, just as we can't say there weren't Latino athletes with the potential to participate in sports at the career level. But having both of these conditions, among others, come together would have been an exceptional case. The example of Jim Thorpe announces this issue clearly. If a Latino or other minority athlete is in the superlative category of physical ability, the chances are that he'll make it. But what of those Latinos who had the *potential* to be an exceptional athlete, another Jim Thorpe, but remained uncultivated? I also come back to the idea of the socioeconomics of this subject. To a working-class Latino family concerned about putting food on the table and purchasing clothes for the children, playing sports might have seemed like a luxury. I think of the men in my family who received scholarship offers to play football at the Division I level and declined the scholarship in order to stay home and earn a paycheck by becoming a welder or oilfield roustabout, say. And this was in the 1980s! Imagine a Latino youth hoping to play professional football in the 1960s or 1970s sitting at the dinner table trying to explain why pursuing a dream that might not pan out was worth taking over staying near the family and earning a living wage by the sweat of one's brow. The kid would be called a dreamer and the discussion would be closed. Perhaps what I'm touching upon

DOI: 10.1057/9781137403094

here has to do with the pragmatics of a career in sports vis-à-vis Latino culture.

FLA: If we travel far enough back in history we see that our participation in football, or something like it, began around 1400 BC. Of course, we weren't tossing around a pig-skinned, ovoid object that characterized the ball in and through the late 19th and early 20th centuries. The Mesoamerican ball game called *ulama* had opposing teams who sought to score a goal by moving (with their hips) a solid rubber ball from one end of the field to the other.

CG: *Ulama* is the oldest known game that involves a rubber ball. As played then, it was definitely intense and most certainly a contact sport. More importantly, I think the very existence of *ulama* runs against this notion that Latinos are somehow a lazy, unathletic people. Just as there are "lazy" individuals in every sort of categorical social group, athleticism isn't the sole domain of one group over another. For the longest time the stereotype of the African American male as the epitome of basketball perfection was often seen as a truism. That is, until basketball went global. After 1992, the Olympic basketball competitions have seen that the American teams, often comprised of African American players, didn't always win the gold medal. So I'm glad you brought up *ulama* as an example from the historical record that Mesoamericans were athletic and very much involved in sport competition.

FLA: Anthropologists have identified that some type of human sacrifice was associated with *ulama*: the decapitation of captives of an antagonistic tribe and/or that of the captain of the losing team.

CG: In other words, *ulama* was more than just a recreational pastime; it was a serious business. And the issue of sacrifice still resonates in the sports world of today. Every time an athlete takes the field or court, there is potential for catastrophic bodily injury. Freak accidents occur out of the blue. Consider Louisville basketball player Kevin Ware's mindboggling leg injury in the 2013 NCAA basketball tournament. He defended a shot as he's probably done thousands upon thousands of times. As he landed, his right leg essentially exploded below the knee. It was horrific, and it happened on a nationally televised game. We take it that basketball isn't really a contact sport the way football is, and still this terrible injury occurred. These athletes put their bodies in harm's way, and often make bodily sacrifices, sacrifices that will impact them long after their playing days are over.

DOI: 10.1057/9781137403094

FLA: Certainly, the modern game of football doesn't involve decapitation. However, players experience much physical damage to the head and other parts of the body. And, proverbial heads roll when a team loses.

CG: The NFL is in a current crisis, and it knows it, regarding the traumatic blows players receive to the head. Despite attempts to make the game safer, there will always be risk of bodily harm in playing this game because of the power and speed of the athletes. The concussion is so dangerous because repeated concussions are cumulative in the damage they do. With each concussion you receive, it could be your last. Former players have claimed debilitating effects they've experienced many years after their playing days were over. Some of these former athletes, such as Dave Duerson, Jovan Belcher, and Junior Seau, have taken their lives by shooting themselves in the heart rather than the head, that their brains might be examined. So, perhaps there are not the violent decapitations that accompanied *ulama* in today's game, but many athletes are experiencing serious adverse effects after having played in the NFL.

FLA: Don DeLillo's lighthearted, comical second novel, *End Zone* (1972) focuses on football in west Texas during its moment of racial integration. The time, space, and narrative voice in the novel seem to intermix issues of race, global politics, and war. Just as there is a war in and around the football and the color line, the narrator also wants to negate the presence of a color line as well as that football is like warfare.

With its hierarchy of segregation as well as divisions from guards to quarterback, the T-formations and running of strategic plays to a coach calling on the sidelines, it's hard *not* to make the analogy between football, institutionalized racism, and militaristic structures and operations…

CG: I grew up in west Texas and southeastern New Mexico, not far from the fabled town of Odessa that inspired *Friday Night Lights*. I went to the same high school as Chicago Bears' linebacker Brian Urlacher (I am a few years older than him). I can attest to the fanaticism of high school football in this area of the country, and I know that other states such as California and Florida boast of equally fervent high school football passion. These high school teams are now as much about the business of winning as many of the top-notch collegiate programs in the country. I live not far from Allen, Texas, a suburb of Dallas, which now boasts a $60 million dollar football stadium for its high school. It was built right in the midst of the Great Recession and opened in the fall of 2012. Thus, in addition to a militaristic type of operation, there is a large measure of

DOI: 10.1057/9781137403094

pride or patriotism that is inherent is such jaw-dropping dollar amounts. High school football tends to answer to no one, and when a community has a tradition of winning, it will invest in continuing that tradition, even if it means other aspects of the high school, namely education, take a back seat.

If we take a wider perspective, though, there is little doubt as to the presence of racism in football. The notion that an African American could not succeed at the position of quarterback, because of its requirements of fast thinking and leadership, is *still* present in the NFL today. Black quarterbacks are held to a higher standard than white quarterbacks, and they are benched much more quickly as well. Warren Moon, an NFL Hall of Famer, had to establish a career in the Canadian Football League (CFL) for six years before the NFL came calling. In 2003, ESPN's failed experiment that incorporated controversial conservative radio talk show host Rush Limbaugh reached its terminus when he claimed that the NFL was propping up Donavan McNabb out of social concern and not that McNabb had earned his position as one of the premiere quarterbacks at the time. One final thing that I'll add points to why the NFL has the so-called Rooney Rule in effect when hiring coaches, which states that a team must include a minority candidate when considering a head coaching or senior coaching hire. There is a reason the Rooney Rule exists: minorities have been historically seen as being incapable of positions of leadership. These matters of race (and sexuality and gender, I might add) are ingrained in the very fabric of organized football, and they will continue to rise to the surface as time goes on.

FLA: Media coverage of football in the late 19th century in venues such as *Harper's Weekly* and *The Nation* identified it as a blood-sport—murderous even.

CG: I think it hearkens back to the bloodlust inherent in spectator sports, the violent underpinnings of these high stakes contests. Just a few years ago there was that *Esquire* cover featuring James Harrison of the Pittsburgh Steelers—notorious for his illegal helmet-to-helmet collisions—shirtless, with a gun in each hand à la the *Hitman* video game cover. ESPN and other sports networks glorify punishing, often illegal hits because it drives up ratings, while at the same time speaking in somber tones whenever a career-ending injury makes its way into the highlight reel.

DOI: 10.1057/9781137403094

FLA: The gladiator pit…

CG: In essence, yes. Empathy for your fellow man can go out the window at an NFL game, and I'm not just talking about the actions on the field among players. It reminds me of the hit Michael Irvin of the Dallas Cowboys took at Veterans Stadium—known simply as The Vet—that ended his career in 1999. There was Irvin, immobile for minutes, until finally the stretcher and cart were brought out, his neck immobilized by a neck brace. Not only was Irvin's career in jeopardy (it proved to be his final game), but his very life was at risk. And yet, through the talk of the announcers on television, you could hear the Philadelphia Eagles crowd *cheering* that Irvin had been wracked with what was clearly a serious injury. Had this occurred in the Colosseum of Rome during the time of Caligula, one would have not been surprised to see the crowd delighting as they gave the thumbs-down signal. Not only do NFL players become a sort of superhuman when they make a team's roster, their humanity oftentimes becomes an afterthought. If they get hurt, even seriously, fans will still complain that their team lost the game as they rush to replace the player on their fantasy team.

FLA: And, oh there is the spectacle of it all. How amazing to be in a stadium with 110,000 people moving in emotional and physical syncopation to the agile movements of skilled athletes making their way up and down the field…

CG: That's the allure of watching the game as a social event, whether at the stadium or at home with friends and family. But in a stadium there is the thrill of watching a play develop. The fans can see it happening and the stadium moves as one. The timing and the coordination of a stellar play not only provide the rush of exhilaration but the play itself lives on in NFL lore. I've seen "The Catch" from Joe Montana to Dwight Clark more times than I can count. We experience the play in the moment and we relive those emotions every time we see the replay. Incidentally, instant replay helped make the NFL such a spectator-friendly sport, even before it helped determine the outcome of actual football games. Watching a televised NFL game, you'll notice that a huge chunk of broadcast time is spent on watching past plays. It helps fill the gap of time between plays while allowing viewers to relive the viewing experience of the play again and again. It happens so frequently that we take the broadcast replays for granted.

DOI: 10.1057/9781137403094

FLA: Might we consider our experience of football to be our modern-day realization of Aristotle's theory of catharsis or purgation as at once the goal and the pleasure of tragedy?

CG: Absolutely. I tend to get so worked up watching an NFL game, even when it involves teams I don't follow, and I'm not alone in this. When watching a game of interest, you are at once exhilarated and frustrated. It is a similar thing we experience in drama or narrative—we ride an emotional rollercoaster, as it were.

FLA: As Aristotle put it, "pity is aroused by unmerited misfortune and fear by the misfortune of a man like ourselves." Perhaps the story of Latino footballers in the NFL whose various journeys invariably bring "unmerited misfortune" and with whom we relate deeply as Latinos arouses intense emotions of pity and fear in us.

CG: Yes, but with one crucial difference. When we see a tragic drama or read a tragic story, we understand, even while suspending our disbelief, that what we are seeing is a construction. It is something *new* in the world—and not an imitation in the strict sense of the word. On the other hand, an NFL game is as close to *mimesis* as we can get, though we understand that the cameras, the replays, the announcers, the sideline reporters, the in-game interviews, and so on are helping to shape the game's narrative. But we as viewers know the game is unscripted, that it might turn suddenly with a botched snap or interception. I've had good friends become angry with me when their team loses, and my Monday can feel absolutely ruined if my team loses the night before.

FLA: Football is about teams, or in-group commonalities, but this necessarily means there is an out-group.

CG: It can't help but divide the groups into an "us vs. them" mentality. Vince Lombardi famously said that winning wasn't everything, it was the *only* thing. The NFL has adopted this mantra to explain the passion and zeal of the game. All things fall subservient to the pursuit of winning. If you're not with us, you're against us, which again aligns with what you said earlier about the military-like structure of the game. Players even use the language of war to describe the game: warrior, battlefield, soldier, captain, and so forth.

FLA: Many things like skin color, accent, language, gender, sexuality, nationality can create differences that solidify out-group and in-group

DOI: 10.1057/9781137403094

divisions. I think of Roberto Clemente's anger with the media of his day that would print soundbites of his in a phonetic English. He hated this because it made him sound illiterate; it made him feel part of the racially targeted out-group.

CG: Ostensibly, football, like all team sports, is supposed to elide differences amongst team members. All team members wear the same uniform and all that. But again, the history of sport in America shows that this does not bear out, and often codified regulations must be adopted before differences in such things as skin color, language, gender, and so on no longer impact a team's dynamic. Clemente was constantly reminded that he was different from the rest of his Pittsburgh Pirates, and he experienced racism of the worst kind in the American South—both because of the color of his skin and his use of English. It's an example that while sports may aspire to a sort of utopian ideal where differences are embraces and valued, the Olympic spirit comes to mind, the reality is that the same sorts of social exigencies that motivate issues of equality also are a part of the sport dynamic as well.

FLA: Yet, we experience an in-group identification when we spot a Latino player on the field...

CG: I think it cannot be helped, especially when Latino players in the NFL are relatively rare. I see a Latino in the NFL and I immediately want to find a shared heritage and experience. Such players become *de facto* representatives of Latino culture, and even the NFL recognizes that. There is a reason Tony González of the Atlanta Falcons is featured in NFL spots celebrating Hispanic Heritage Month during the month of September. Savvy NFL marketers know that Latinos will identify with someone like González, and they hope such Latino players will create a lasting fan base amongst Latinos. As the sheer numbers of Latinos continues to rise in the U.S., along with their spending power, the NFL wants more Latinos to identify with the game. Again, it is smart business.

FLA: As the history of Latinos in the NFL proves, more often than not our in-group and out-group differentiation can have negative consequences.

CG: Two very recent examples may help illustrate how negative these consequences you allude to can be. The first takes me back to the 2013 NBA Finals that featured the Miami Heat versus the San Antonio Spurs.

DOI: 10.1057/9781137403094

It should go without saying that Latinos are fervent fans of the Spurs because of the geographical location of the city and the population of Latinos who live in San Antonio. (Incidentally, a similar argument might be made of the Heat and the strong Cuban-American base of fans in Miami.) Nevertheless, Game 3 showcased a young Mexican-American named Sebastien de la Cruz, an eleven-year-old mariachi singer who dazzled the judges on *America's Got Talent* just a year earlier. De la Cruz gave a strong rendition of the "Star-Spangled Banner" in the pregame ceremonies, and Twitter exploded with racist outrage for the young singer. Despite his status as American, many Twitter users wanted to know why a "Mexican" was singing the American anthem. He was instantly seen as belonging to the out-group, and the result was a disgusting display of racist hatred for a talented young singer.

Similarly, just one month later in July 2013, noted pop singer Marc Anthony sang "God Bless America" during the seventh-inning stretch of the MLB All-Star Game. Just as with Sebastien de la Cruz, the Internet outrage was overwhelming. The same sorts of insults were hurled at Anthony, such as, "Why is a Mexican singing our national anthem?" despite the fact that Anthony is Puerto Rican, meaning he is an American citizen. So, just as Latinos might identify with a Latino as belonging to the same in-group, there are equal numbers of individuals who want to make Latinos as an out-group. Here we see the "us vs. them" applied to whole groups of people. They might say, this is *our* anthem, this is *our* sport. If this is going on now, how can we think that this sort of out-grouping of Latinos hasn't impacted the number of Latinos in, say, the NFL?

FLA: In *Understanding Nationalism* Patrick Colm Hogan specifies the precise emotion systems involved in categorial identification and in-group/out-group division. For Hogan, categorial identity is what one takes to be definitive labels for one's essence, labels for the sets that define who one is. It is well established that we form in-groups and out-groups, and thus categorial identity divisions, very easily. Even in contexts where they are temporary, such divisions can have very striking consequences. According to Hogan, they lead us to judge members of the in-group more favorably, to prefer the relative superiority of the in-group over absolute higher benefits for everyone, and so on. That is, they can lead one to valorize internal group hierarchies. I wonder if this insight can help us understand better the lack of Latinos in the NFL.

DOI: 10.1057/9781137403094

CG: As long as Latinos are viewed as an out-group, they will struggle to be seen as a viable member of the NFL. They'll be seen as pretenders playing a game that's not their own. Or, because Latinos are seen as more passionate about soccer, the greatest concentration of Latino players has tended to be, until relatively recently, placekickers and punters. It will take more Latino athletes in the NFL—in a host of skilled positions—to solidify Latinos as an in-group within the hierarchy of football.

FLA: Let's recall those master narratives that continue to circulate today: Latinos are not built for sports like football (as opposed to African Americans whose history of surviving against the odds as enslaved led to the evolution of a preternatural strength). Latinos are lazy and undisciplined. Latinos are dumb....

CG: Jimmy Snyder, known as Jimmy the Greek, was famously dumped by CBS in 1988 after asserting that African American players were physically better because of the breeding that occurred during American slavery. And yet, those types of master narratives still fester in many aspects of American sports. Latinos have been erroneously categorized as having small and squat frames, or that they are too slow (both physically and intellectually). Latinos like soccer, so let's make them kickers! And yet, someone like Hall of Famer Anthony Muñoz comes along and helps redefine the position of tackle. Or Tony Casillas. Or Tony González. Or Victor Cruz. It takes the hard work of these types of Latinos to break stereotypical ideas of how successful Latinos can be in the NFL.

FLA: Football is physically demanding—and a very physical game to watch. On the field we see the clash of oppositional teams. We await a victor. We perceive physical movement and experience tremendous emotions, often conflictive, as the game unfolds. We jump from our seats with upset, surprise, and happiness even. The discovery of our mirror neuron system helps explain all this. This networked area of our brain lights up with action both when we actually physically *do* something that is action oriented (like throw, kick, or catch a ball) and when we watch others *do* something that is action oriented (like throw, kick, or catch a ball). That is, they enable us to simulate in our brain the agentful action of others. This has led us to understand better how things like empathy work, but it might also shed light on why football is such a successful spectacle sport. We don't and can't focus on all the players at once, but we can on one or two doing the action. (The game seems to move forward

DOI: 10.1057/9781137403094

through a series of gaps that allow us to distinguish player into clusters of bodies that collapse our capacity to distinguish one from the other.) We invest in these players perceptually and emotionally. Of course, if you are like us and attend to the Latinos on the field, these will be the agentful subjects that trigger our mirror neurons.

CG: I am sometimes embarrassed when I hear my wife describe me watching a football game. I'm often not aware of the fact that I am groaning or yelling, or that I've suddenly begun jumping around like a maniac as a play unfolds. Likewise, it is the agony I seem to feel when a crucial catch is not completed. As I mentioned earlier, the advent of replay seems to heighten the emotional triggers you discuss above. NFL fans have certain players they identify with, for whatever reason, and a Latino watching Tony González make a spectacular catch might feel a greater emotive response because he is seen as belonging to the same in-group. Likewise, children want to emulate their favorite players. They see someone with a similar surname, a similar look, and they now believe that they can achieve a similar level of success as well. It is why role models are so crucial to young people, and minorities in particular.

FLA: In *What Literature Teaches Us about Emotion*, Hogan distinguishes between empathy and emotion contagion. The initial, spontaneous simulation of emotion is presumably closer to contagion. But it is probably a necessary condition for empathy proper.

CG: I'm not sure how empathy factors into something like a football game, but I can see that emotion contagion would be very much a part of the spectator experience. To have an entire group of people, perhaps as large as tens of thousands of spectators, simultaneously experience the same sort of emotions, is an impressive thing to behold.

FLA: Perhaps the Greeks were on to something with their concept of *Agôn*: the state of mind and emotions that spin out of our experience (vicarious or otherwise) of a clash of opposing forces that often occurs during athletic competitions (the body *going beyond* itself) and that, for the Greeks anyway, led to our growth.

CG: I think so, and it demonstrates just how little has changed in terms of how we engage with spectator sports since the time of the ancient Greeks. As an audience, we delight in the physical abilities of these athletes who are at the pinnacle of human achievement. Perhaps this is hero

DOI: 10.1057/9781137403094

worship to some extent, but it is certainly a manifestation of participating in these extraordinary achievements vicariously or by proxy. We buy the football jerseys and follow our favorite players' every move because their glory falls upon us as well. It is quite easy to get swept up in the emotion of it all.

FLA: The football game moves in a series of pulses of expanding and shrinking time and space that radically differ from, say, that of baseball with its stretched out and idle time/space, making it all the more important for us to zero in on the Latino as agentful body...

CG: Not only is the concept of time a distinguishing characteristic of football, but the very issue of timing is crucial for the success or failure of any given team. Each offensive player knows exactly where they are supposed to be and when they are supposed to be there, while the defense is constantly trying to anticipate these scripted moves. At any given moment you have 22 men on the field, all coordinated one way or the other.

FLA: After discussing the erotics of *fútbol* (1982 World Cup in Barcelona) in *Making Waves*, Mario Vargas Llosa is careful not to over idealize it as a space of freedom and equality. Rather, he is careful to remind us that it exists in a world filled with inequality, lawlessness, and violence. Yet, he also considers that *fútbol* (or soccer) "offers people something that they can scarcely ever have: an opportunity to have fun, to enjoy themselves, to get excited, worked up, to feel certain intense emotions that daily routine rarely offers them."...

CG: Speaking of getting worked up, I marvel at how devastating a loss can be for the passionate football fan. I'm sure dogs have been kicked, televisions have been broken, and doors slammed all as a consequence of getting worked up over a game. I have found myself angered at the outcome of certain games, disgusted with one player's performance, perhaps. And then I remind myself that this is a game that is essentially played amongst millionaires. I'm the one losing sleep over a loss, and yet the player gets to go home to his multi-million dollar mansion. Some people may go so far as to riot and loot, even after a great victory! There is undoubtedly an emotional investment in a NFL sports fan that is unlike other types of experienced emotions. We may not know what it's like to win the Super Bowl, but we can cheer as if we had when our favorite team hoists the Lombardi trophy at season's end.

DOI: 10.1057/9781137403094

1

From Scrimmage Lines to End Zones: Latinos in the National Football League

Abstract: *"A Question of the Brown* Scrimmage *Line,"* *provides a nuanced socio-cultural analysis of exclusionary practices and trends in the early history of the pro leagues—or what the authors identify as the brown color line.*

Frederick Luis Aldama and Christopher González. *Latinos in the End Zone: Conversations on the Brown Color Line in the NFL.* New York: Palgrave Macmillan, 2014.
DOI: 10.1057/9781137403094.

Frederick Luis Aldama: Christopher, we could go back several millennia but the plot of Latinos in football doesn't become caught up in extremes till the moment when it becomes codified as a professional sport in 1920 when it was identified as the American Professional Football League (APFL).

Christopher González: It really is the place to begin when discussing the sport as a professional endeavor, though the APFL would become the NFL only two years later. However, we'd be remiss if we didn't at least acknowledge two key innovators that predate 1920. Fabled Notre Dame Fighting Irish coach Knute Rockne is noted for developing and popularizing a key development of American football, a development that would distinguish it from its cousin rugby—the forward pass. It's hard to imagine the game we know today without a quarterback throwing the football down the field, but that's how the game was initially designed. When Rockne instituted the forward pass, the game essentially became what we know today, though there would be minor adjustments along the way. The other innovator is Glenn "Pop" Warner, a prolific and successful early coach—and coach of Jim Thorpe—who among other things innovated the now familiar play called the screen. Today his legacy is in the "Pop Warner" programs that begin to develop football players at a very early age. Though these two men shaped the game at the collegiate level, their contributions began to make their way into the professional game. But for our purposes, we'll begin at 1920.

FLA: While racial prejudice and segregation practices meant that Latinos would not appear in the AFL till the 1930s, it's worth recalling that football during this period and before still carried the marker of being a rough, working-class game.

CG: It has certainly never been what we might call a safe sport. Football's early years were marked with many serious (some fatal) injuries to players, and a constant tweaking to the rules was initiated, a tweaking that has never stopped. But by the 1930s the game had now become very close to what we know today, and the decade was marked with a settling of the foundation upon which the NFL would build itself into the premiere commercial sports league in the U.S., if not the world.

FLA: Just as its cousin rugby was not the venerated sport of the bourgeoisie (tennis, golf, polo), neither was football. Moreover, it was a sport that inhabited a kind of borderland: as neither soccer nor rugby but a hybrid combination of both that made something new. Many an athletic pundit and others viewed it with suspicion.

DOI: 10.1057/9781137403094

CG: It's hard to believe it now, in a time when football is such a ratings and economic juggernaut, but in its early years football was essentially a boorish sport. And it was so out of necessity. We're talking about a full contact sport with only minimal protective gear. The advent of the protective facemask was many years away, and the thin leather headgear egregiously called a helmet was the extent of protection. Broken noses and lost teeth were all too common. Seen in the light of the more passive type sports such as tennis and golf, an observer of the NFL's early years might have thought the players were just simply not going to last that long. In truth, even in today's game the pro career averages less than ten years before players are compelled to retire either because of diminishing skills, or more often, as a result of injury.

FLA: Oddly, while it was certainly not tennis or golf, this hybrid was played at elite universities like Yale and Princeton, Harvard, Tuft, Rutgers, Columbia—all of which had formed football associations in the middle of the 19th century.

CG: As I suggested earlier, the development and proliferation of football in the college ranks really was the impetus for the NFL. As you note, Frederick, these universities were playing an early form of football for over 50 years before the APFL appeared. To put that into perspective, that's longer than the current Super Bowl era of the NFL. (There have been 42 Super Bowls as of the writing of this book.) These college football programs—many in the Ivy League—in many ways helped shape the development of the game of football.

It's an interesting thing to note this early connection between football and higher education. In this case, we're talking about *the* premier universities of the time. So, even though the game may have had a workingman's ethos about it, the men who played it at the collegiate level were the sons of America's captains of industry. But already we can see these barriers of entry during the inception of game of football. Not just anyone was going to get into Yale or Harvard, and thus not just anyone could play on these collegiate teams.

FLA: By the time of the early 20th century when professional athletic clubs began to give football a formal presence in the sportsworld, it was already in the shadow of an established pro baseball.

CG: And it might have very well stayed in baseball's shadow but for one crucial technical innovation: television. I have the feeling we'll discuss the issue of television and how it changed the NFL forever, but for now

DOI: 10.1057/9781137403094

let me just say that between the two games—baseball and football— football is designed perfectly for the medium of television. The NFL is a ratings behemoth, and the Super Bowl is perennially the highest rated television show of any given year. So, while football may have been at a disadvantage early on, it was propelled to stratospheric heights once games became televised.

FLA: The game seems plagued from the outset with all variety of contradictions: working class identified and a marginal sport (banned even for a spell for its violence in the 1860s) yet it was played by WASPs (sons) of elite families at elite universities.

CG: I think you're absolutely spot on. It does seem like a contradiction. On the one hand you have roughneck types playing this contact sport, but it was also a sport that emanated from the ivory towers of American academia. That contradiction might be resolved if we examine how the game went from East coast elite universities, migrated to the Midwest, and ended up in Central Ohio. Right around the time the young NFL began to solidify in terms of its teams, the college game spread to universities in all areas of the country. It was during this "Ohio League" time of the game's development that the working-class nature of the game came to fore. Smaller cities surrounding Columbus, such as Canton, became early stalwarts of the NFL. This was an important transition for the game, but because players were still selected from institutions of higher learning, the issues of access we've discussed already were in place since the inception of the professional game.

FLA: Of course, universities like Yale, Harvard, Princeton today are not known for their football, as it became more popular in college in its nascent days, universities would use their football puissance as a marker of distinction.

CG: Without question it is the reason Notre Dame was able to become such a name-brand institution. Knute Rockne was a maestro on the gridiron, and it was football that gave that puissance you mentioned to universities like Notre Dame. The University of Michigan also became an immense powerhouse in collegiate football's early days, and they won the first ever Rose Bowl, crushing Stanford 49–0. Collegiate football programs spread down the Atlantic coast and through the South,

DOI: 10.1057/9781137403094

and across the Midwest. And again, we can't ever seem to leave the issue of economics when it comes to this particular sport. Football was (and is) a revenue dynamo. So while its early years might have been marked with ivory-tower distinction, it soon demonstrated a different kind of elitism—in this case, big time revenue streams. Money talks, as they say.

FLA: Today, public, land-grant universities such as OSU where I teach and that should be recruiting top-shelf Latino students (athletes or otherwise) seem to care more about sustaining a self-enclosed, self-feeding, self-fattening football revenue stream.

CG: The irony of the economics of college football is either disheartening or frustrating. Anyone who is involved in college football must be suffering from a fair amount of cognitive dissonance. On the one hand you have a governing body such as the NCAA whose sole purpose these days seems to be to sanction football programs whose players make side money for talents produced by their own bodies. On the other hand, the NCAA and top-tier university football programs generate an enormous amount of wealth on the backs of these students. It is a controversy that rages consistently, though it may wax and wane depending on who the latest culprit may be. Every televised game, every t-shirt with a school logo, every bit of memorabilia and merchandise feeds this football economic system. Though the NCAA often touts itself as the last bastion of pure amateurism in a cold, cruel professional world, the truth is that college football, like its cousin the NFL, is a business where fortunes are won and lost. When you think of top-notch college football programs as Fortune 500-types of businesses, suddenly what they do makes complete sense. But if one views these programs as subservient to institutions of higher education, well, then the lens is certainly rose-colored indeed.

FLA: While elite universities continued to open doors only for privileged WASPS, those like OSU and neighboring universities like Oberlin were actually breaking color lines. Not with Latinos, but with African Americans. I think of Oberlin's early streak with putting on the football field African American players such as William Washington (1897–1899), Samual Samuel Morrell (1901 to 1902), and Nathanial Brown (1908–1909). In the 1920s an NFL club in Akron, Ohio, championed the African American running back, Frederick Douglas "Fritz" Pollard.

DOI: 10.1057/9781137403094

CG: It's interesting that you mention Ohio. Not only is the Buckeye State of key importance to the bourgeoning days of the NFL, but it remains the centerpoint for producing one of the most important barrier-smashing athletes in all of American history: Jesse Owens. On the world's stage he, a Black man, made Adolf Hitler look like an utter buffoon with his nonsense of a superior Aryan race. The world owes Jesse Owens thanks for that, if nothing else.

But to have such progressive institutions and forward-thinking attitudes on race in Ohio makes perfect sense when you consider the state's history with race. For many slaves, Ohio was the land of freedom. Crossing the Ohio River was like a baptism and being born again, only this time as a whole human being. I don't mean to oversimplify the issue; there were certainly barriers for minorities even in a state such as Ohio. But, if we were to introduce a hypothetical here, what if these early football clubs had flourished in, say, Birmingham, Alabama? Would we have seen the likes of a William Washington or Nathanial Brown, in a state that still proudly claimed its segregation provenance as late as 1963?

FLA: Likely not, Christopher. Indeed, while there were pockets of emancipation in the game, at some point in the early 20th century it became the common doxa for coaches to take the position that there weren't any players of color to recruit.

CG: Such a doxa works especially well when there are few players of color to recruit. I just mentioned Alabama's sad history of segregation. If in 1963 President John F. Kennedy has to mobilize National Guard troops in order to allow a handful of African American students into the University of Alabama, of course football coaches around the same time would throw up their hands and say, "Well, we tried!" If the institution itself didn't allow a segregated student body, what chance did any student of color (football player or otherwise) have? I appear to be concentrating on the University of Alabama's infamy, but there were hundreds of institutions doing the same thing in the first half of the 20th century in America. In 1962 the University of Mississippi, or Ole Miss, had a much more devastating, but similar, situation when James Meredith became the first African American student on campus. At the same time we're looking at an NFL that was already four decades old, with the Super Bowl era just around the corner, and schools such as the University of Alabama and Ole Miss *don't even have minority students enrolled in classes!*

DOI: 10.1057/9781137403094

One final hypothetical before moving on. If the NFL, instead of rooting itself in Ohio, had decided to establish itself in Texas, perhaps centered in San Antonio, how many Latinos would we have in the early years of the NFL? I speculate that we'd have had many more than the archive now shows.

FLA: When Latinos and Native Americans were finally added to the roster of pro football teams, like their Black counterparts they weren't allowed to dress or eat with their white teammates or even stay in the same hotel.

CG: Talk about in-group/out-group! It's hard to feel like you belong to a team when you're not treated in the same way. You mentioned Roberto Clemente earlier, Frederick, and he was essentially treated as both a Latino and as an African American. If he wasn't "damned" because of his dark skin, he was "damned" because of his heavily accented English. It's stunning that Clemente was able to become one of the greatest MLB players of all time when one considers the added stress and frustration he felt because of such entrenched racism. When minority athletes began making it into the upper echelons of sport, they constantly had the burden of proving that they had as much right to belong as white athletes. The treatment of African American quarterbacks in the NFL is a prime example of this. Athletes always feel as if they have something to prove, in general; it comes with being an athlete. But minority athletes in a segregated society could only produce spectacular athletic feats or they would be dumped at the first poor performance they had.

FLA: During these early days when we began to see more players of color in the football leagues. One of the most significant players to cross the color line in Ohio (Canton Bulldogs) was Wa-Tho-Huk from Oklahoma. Of course, most know him as Jim Thorpe (1888–1953)—another assimilation move, right?

CG: Thorpe, as I mentioned in the Prologue, was an athlete for the ages. No matter to which race or ethnicity he had belonged, he was going to be a nearly superheroic athlete. Thorpe was able to cross the color line, as you put it, though his parents were, like Thorpe himself, of mixed Native and European ancestry. Because he was of mixed heritage, growing up close to his Native culture in Prague, Oklahoma, he was better able to make the transition into a sport world dominated by whites.

DOI: 10.1057/9781137403094

Thorpe's life is utterly fascinating, and I think fewer and fewer people remember Jim Thorpe these days. I think today's culture tends to reach to its recent past when naming the great athletes. Today it's all about Michael Jordan and LeBron James. That aside, it's curious to see how Jim Thorpe's legacy is handled today. Phenotypically, there is no question that he has Native American features. I suggested earlier that had Thorpe insisted on being called Wa-Tho-Huk, people would view him and the NFL quite differently today. But he's "Jim Thorpe," and if you can manage ignoring the occasional black and white photo of him, a person might think of Thorpe as a white man without a significant Native tradition in his genes. James Fennimore Cooper created his famous Natty Bumppo (aka, Deerslayer, aka, Hawkeye) character as a white man who had adopted the best of Native culture, and the NFL seemingly took a Native man and gave him the best of white culture. They took the greatest athlete of the 20th century, according to many, and "whitewashed" him. That's not to say they didn't acknowledge his Native ancestry. Rather, they treat it as an "oh-by-the-way" footnote.

FLA: Thorpe story certainly inspires, but it's not without its tragic aspects. I mean, he was of that generation of Native Americans that was schooled with the express purpose of assimilating into the dominant white culture. At the schools he attended like Carlisle Indian Industrial School and the Haskell Indian Junior College, like academic subjects such as English and History, American sports like football and baseball were used to assimilate Native Americans.

CG: The sad thing is that these Native American kids were losing their culture under the guise of playing a game, though it must have been evident to the adults. Glenn "Pop" Warner, football coach at Carslile, and Thorpe's coach, often used the White vs. Indian history of conflict in order to motivate his Native American players, employing racially loaded terms in order to get his message across. Warner famously is quoted as saying, "Trick plays were what the redskins loved best. Nothing delighted them more than to outsmart the palefaces." And this was the *coach* at Carslile, who ostensibly had his players' best interests in mind.

FLA: Ironically, Thorpe proved his football prowess on a team called the "Indians" and then after playing (earning $250 a game) for the Canton Bulldogs (1915–1917; 1919–1920), he went on to play with other teams that included the Cleveland Indians ...

DOI: 10.1057/9781137403094

CG: It marks the early but highly influential beginning of the shameful practice of making Native Americans into sports mascots.

FLA: While there were a few more players of color in the 1920s and 1930s, we seemed to see an increasing interest in using Native American names as team mascots (the Fill-in-the-Blank Indians and of course later the Washington Redskins). On the one hand, educational, judicial, public policies seemed hell bent on erasing (destroying or assimilating) Others; and on the other hand, there was this fascination at the level of symbol.

CG: It's another form of minstrelsy—using a caricature of a marginalized social group as a means of creating entertainment for whites. After all, Native Americans had little power to stop these embarrassing uses of their people as a symbol, and all we have to do is look to the present day. One would think that our society had evolved enough of a social conscience that we wouldn't have "Redskins" as a mascot of an NFL team or the ever-grinning Chief Wahoo as mascot of the Cleveland Indians. But even today, because there is so much money invested in these two teams in particular, as well as others who generally employ a Native American mascot, no lobby is powerful enough to make the teams change their mascot. And the reason? As the character Yogurt (Mel Brooks) said in the movie *Spaceballs*, "Merchandising! Merchandising!" It's branding in more ways than one.

FLA: We think this discrimination is a nightmare from bygone days, but just take a look at the Pro Football Hall of Fame. This is an institution located in a state (Ohio) with a track record of being less prejudiced toward players of color, yet it continues to prove to be a xenophobic gatekeeper.

CG: We must keep in mind that the repository for the Hall of Fame—the building, the busts, the memorabilia, rests in Canton, Ohio, but the Selection Committee for who gets into the Hall of Fame is not located in Ohio. The committee, at present a 46-member body, is essentially comprised of media figures who cover the regional action of the NFL. So, those who choose what stories to write about and which players to focus on also determine who ultimately goes into the Hall of Fame. There are many deserving players who are still waiting, and many inductees that are somewhat headscratchers. Former players, unlike the National Baseball Hall of Fame, do not help select inductees. I think it shows how media driven the NFL ultimately is—that the media literally dictates who is worthy of the Hall of Fame.

DOI: 10.1057/9781137403094

FLA: Let's return to Latinos in the Hall of Fame later in our conversation. I'd like to return to Thorpe for a minute. Some argue that his extraordinary athletic prowess and showman-like skills propelled football into the realm of spectacle; a spectacle, that is, that would go on to become the billion dollar enterprise it is today. Yet, his story ends in tragedy. Thorpe died with a few pennies in his pocket and psoriasis of the liver …

CG: When you bring up this issue, instantly I see Lyle Alzado's face, his bald, cancer-ridden head wrapped in a "do-rag," on the cover of *Sports Illustrated* with the words "I LIED" in huge letters. He would die shortly thereafter at the age of 43. He was in the midst of a comeback, and I can still remember watching, with my brother, footage on T.V. of Alzado training like a madman for his return to the NFL. Then suddenly, he became this frail little man, not the awesome player I remembered. He was dying, and he was going to let everyone know why he believed his brain cancer was the result of drug use. He exposed the heavy use of PEDs in the NFL, and predictably, the organization assumed no culpability. Would that Alzado was an outlier. But the fact is that many NFL players have died before their time, without NFL's support in their dying days.

Tragically, it is an all-too-common theme with the NFL. It's strange that the NFL, a sport-as-entertainment enterprise, and "professional wrestling," which markets itself as entertainment posing as sport, have a litany of athletes who have died too soon. I'll concentrate on the NFL, but anyone familiar with the WWE understands what I'm talking about. Again, I think we're keen to remember that the NFL is first and foremost a business. It tends to protect its investment (i.e., players) as much as it can, but it also wants to entertain the fanbase, which thrives on big plays and devastating hits. We witness a crushing hit and see the players pop up and return to the huddle, ready for the next play, and think, "Hey, he's okay!" But the cumulative effect of these hits takes a toll on the bodies of these players. The NFL Players Association is seemingly in constant battle with the NFL regarding post-career compensation and medical benefits of former players. The NFL is very much "now" oriented. It is interested in the popularity of the sport and revenue dollars, now. It is less interested in the consequences of the punishment the sport of professional football delivers to exceptional, but all too human bodies.

FLA: Along with the Native American Thorpe were Latinos that helped turn football into a money-making spectacle sport. When the Rodríguez

DOI: 10.1057/9781137403094

brothers Jesse and Kelly got into the pro football game in 1929 they stunned audiences with their extraordinary long distance punts. The Buffalo Bisons showcased Jesse in punting exhibitions. They also surprised crowds with their David-Goliath techniques. Like his brother, Kelly was relatively small in build (5 feet 10 inches or so) but as quarterback and running back, could defeat the biggest of players when playing for the Frankford (Philadelphia) Yellowjackets and the Minneapolis Redjackets.

CG: During those early years of the professional game there was less stereotyping in terms of who could play what position than there was in later years. But even in the example of the Rodríguez brothers, they are noted for their exceptional ability to kick the football. I'm sure we'll discuss this later on, but Latinos seem to have a preternatural ability to kick, or at least that's how it seems. That Kelly and Jesse had small frames and were permitted to play the position of quarterback tells you all you need to know about that era of the game. Quarterback Doug Flutie, whose famous "Hail Mary" pass while at Boston College is now a part of football lore, and who, retired in 2005, expressed his frustration at the discrimination he constantly experienced in his career because of his height. He is exactly the same height as Kelly Rodríguez at 5 feet 10 inches. Kelly and Jesse would have had little opportunity to play quarterback in a later era, and that's without considering their Latino heritage as a potential factor. But the fact that they *did* play is an important fact in the historical record.

FLA: The 1940s was not a good decade for football—and even less so for Latinos in football. With the exception of Joe Aguirre (1918–1985) who was drafted out of St. Mary's College (California) in 1941 to play tight end for the Washington Redskins, the U.S. participation in World War II put the brakes on the game ... for everyone.

CG: It was inevitable. When the country rationed resources, when entertainers were drafted into service, when professional baseball players left the team to fight for Uncle Sam, even the NFL was going to feel the effects of war. Now, clearly the NFL of the 1940s was not the NFL during, say, the most recent wars in Iraq and Afghanistan in terms of its economic viability. But the war effort did restrict the growth of football for many years.

FLA: "Lupe Joe" Arenas (1925–) attended the University of Nebraska on the GI Bill then went on to play with the 49ers as a kicker and punt

DOI: 10.1057/9781137403094

returner (1951–1957). Dare we say that one of the positive consequences of the war was that it offered Latinos the possibility of going to college on the GI Bill—and for those interested in football, the chance to sharpen skills to enter the pro leagues?

CG: I don't think there is any doubt as to how important the GI Bill was for many Latinos who were interested in higher education. And since we've already made the case that Latinos would have to gain admittance into these institutions if they were ever to find a career in the NFL, the GI Bill has to be seen as an important development. On the other hand, your brief description of Lupe Joe is another reminder of the types of positions Latinos often played in the NFL (kicker). But Arenas was also punt returner, which is a dynamic position that requires courage, speed, and agility even above other positions.

FLA: At the same time, during the 1950s we begin to see many Latinos (Joe Aguirre included) crossing the border to play for Canadian Football League teams like Winnipeg Blue Bombers, the Edmonton Eskimos, Saskatchewan Roughriders, for instance … Often this was a back door for Latinos to play in the NFL …

CG: The CFL was a backdoor for many players. The aforementioned Doug Flutie and Warren Moon, and many others spent many years playing in Canada before making the roster of an NFL team. Unfortunately in the U.S., the Canadian brand of football is seen as second-tier, which I think might be debatable. They play a different style, just as arena-league football has a different style, and a difference of style necessitates a different skill set.

FLA: One of the more famous Latino players during this period was Tom Fears (1922–2000) who was drafted, trained as a pilot (to get over to fight the Japanese who had captured his father), played football for a service team in Colorado Springs, then after the war attended UCLA on the GI Bill. In 1948 the Los Angeles Rams drafted him as a receiver; after playing for the Rams till 1956) he became an assistant coach to the Rams, the Packers, the Falcons and then head coach to New Orleans Saints (1967–1970) among others. What do we do with this mindful of contradictions that seem to envelope the lives of these early players: war (therefore murder) and education (therefore opportunity).

DOI: 10.1057/9781137403094

CG: Any potential player who had military training, and in the case of Fears, pilot training, was like a stamp of approval for all of the traits an organization like the NFL would find desirable—leadership, discipline, courage, and so on. But Fears is an interesting case in that he was born in Mexico, but like Thorpe, was of mixed ancestry. His father was a white American; his mother was Mexican.

You mention the contradictions here, but the more I think of it the more it seems that the NFL and war have made interesting bedfellows. Recall the "us vs. them" mentality; the sort of language used by Pop Warner that invoked the U.S. Army vs. Native Americans; the kind of language used by players, even today, that invoke warlike imagery; the incredible story of Pat Tillman, who after 9/11 renounced his life as an NFL star for the Arizona Cardinals in order to join the Army Rangers, and would later die under suspicious circumstances in Afghanistan; and much more. Perhaps it's not so strange to see these periodic but significant connections between the military and football after all.

FLA: When you look over the roster of early Latino players in the NFL the majority seem to have been brought on as kickers. I'm not just thinking of the Bros Rodríguez. But of players like: "Lupe Joe" Arenas (1925–) who played 7 seasons for 49ers as a kicker and punt returner (1951–1957). Rick Jose Casares (1931–) that made records for kick-off returns and rushing yardage when he played for the Bears (1955–1960). And, while Eddie Sáenz (1923–1971) played halfback and defensive back, he became best known as kick returner for the Redskins (1946–1951), consistently leading in kick-off return yardage during this time. I know that in its earlier incarnation, kicking played a more significant role in the game, but I do wonder if in these early days of Latino presence in the game if there was something more than coincidence at work here.

CG: I've been hinting (not so subtly) to this moment, and I'm glad we can finally address the issue head on. If I wanted to put it in the best possible light, I'd say that many of these Latino players were adept at kicking because they had played soccer before becoming kickers in football. In the early years of the game the football was kicked straight on, whereas in later years so-called soccer style kicking became the norm, and it is the style of kicking we see in the game today. However, there is an inordinate number of Latinos who have become kickers in the game of football, and

DOI: 10.1057/9781137403094

they can't all have been soccer virtuosos. And that's what convinces me that all this is more than coincidence.

Remember that I mentioned the issue of stereotyping certain kinds of players as fitting certain roles or positions over others. Football is a conservative game in its philosophy; it dislikes experimentation and risk (except when it works!), and it tends to rely on predictable plays that are statistically successful at specific moments and situations in the game. We see head coaches today with color coordinated, laminated sheets that designate which plays to call in certain downs and distance. Also, recall that when Mike Ditka used William "the Refrigerator" Perry as a running back in a game, it was denounced as a gimmick. The history of the game shows that players with certain physical attributes are best suited to play certain positions. If you're too short, like the Rodríguez brothers or Doug Flutie, you may never play the position you truly want to play, such as quarterback. And even if you do, you may constantly be told you're not good enough.

At some point, even a well-meaning coach might see a Latino player and automatically think the player is best suited to be a kicker. It shouldn't surprise anyone that players are stereotyped in a game that spends millions of dollars a year stereotyping players. Only they call it "scouting."

FLA: Eddie Sáenz was called "Tortilla" on the field ...

CG: He was called "Tortilla" for no other reason than he was Latino. Like calling an African American player "Watermelon," it's demonstrative of the sort of racist thinking that pervades American sports. And "Tortilla" is what Sáenz was called publicly. We can only imagine the sorts of names he was called outside of the public's earshot.

DOI: 10.1057/9781137403094

2
From Punishing Penalties to Brown Bodies Raiding the NFL

Abstract: *"From Punishing Penalties to Brown Bodies Raiding the NFL" considers several significant moments when Latinos broke through the brown color line, including the pivotal moment when two of the NFL's most significant Latino figures Tom Flores (coach) and Jim Plunkett (quarterback) took the Raiders to two Super Bowl victories.*

Frederick Luis Aldama and Christopher González. *Latinos in the End Zone: Conversations on the Brown Color Line in the NFL*. New York: Palgrave Macmillan, 2014. DOI: 10.1057/9781137403094.

Frederick Luis Aldama: As we've already begun to show, the story of Latinos in pro football interweaves with the history of struggle of other racial minorities in football. We talked about Thorpe, but there were important black players like Ozzie Simmons, Lou Montgomery, Leonard Bates, and Kenny Washington who dared challenge—and cross the color line as far as possible. In spite of being UCLA's leading ground gainer, Washington was barred from playing in the College All-Star game (1939), for instance.

Christopher González: We ended the last chapter by mentioning how Eddie Sáenz was called "Tortilla." Ozzie Simmons was called the "Ebony Eel," and I'm not sure if that's any better. But Simmons was originally from Texas, and his school was segregated, as one would expect in the late 1920s and early 1930s. One of the things we've only hinted at, Frederick, is that schools for minorities in the segregated education system had far fewer resources than their white counterparts. For someone like Simmons, imagine the sort of disadvantages he faced as a student when he entered the University of Iowa. Imagine the kind of academic catching up he had to do through no fault of his own. Simmons is emblematic of the early NFL in that he was not allowed to play professionally because he was African American, and by the time he *was* permitted to play, his career was over in a couple of years.

Lou Montgomery just recently received recognition for the racism he endured as a player at Boston College. Like Simmons, Montgomery was the first African American player in the history of his university's football program, and opposing teams would refuse to take the field if Montgomery played, a policy known as the "gentleman's agreement." Instead of standing up for their players of color, teams would acquiesce if the opposing team protested—yet another reminder of the misnomer of "team" in those days and a further illustration of in-group/out-group dynamics.

Boston College honored Montgomery in 2012 by retiring his jersey, albeit posthumously. Leonard Bates, like Montgomery, was forced to sit on the bench in very important games, and forward-thinking students protested these racist policies at NYU in 1941, and those students received severe sanctions for leading peaceful protests in support of Bates. And only in 2001, begrudgingly, did NYU apologize for these outrages. And you note what happened to Kenny Washington.

DOI: 10.1057/9781137403094

FLA: Latinos were also kept out of the white locker rooms; and during team trips that some were allowed to go on, they were not allowed to cohabitate with the white players.

CG: It's the sort of paradoxical "othering" that leaves me bewildered. A player of color is deemed worthy enough to take the field with his white counterparts, but those same players can't use the same locker room or eat at the same restaurants as their white teammates. It goes against everything I've ever experienced in sports. There is supposed to be a camaraderie between teammates, a "band of brothers" mentality. (There we go with another war metaphor, this time courtesy of Shakespeare.) To be *a part of* a group while being *apart from* the group must have been so difficult for those early barrier breaking players.

FLA: Of course, one of the issues that has been discussed by academics generally is that Latinos have historically fallen through the cracks in a country that sees the race problem as only Black and White. Certainly, our demographic numbers were smaller during this earlier epoch than they are today. However, one can't but reason that any move forward for others discriminated against in the leagues must have been a step forward for Latinos.

CG: Latino athletes in professional football and baseball owe a huge debt to those players who had the courage to hurtle past the barriers of racism in sports. Racism has impacted Latinos differently than African Americans, true, but the two groups share the characteristic of being labeled as "non-white." Jackie Robinson and Willie Mays helped pave the way for Roberto Clemente. Could Clemente have piled up his successes without the path carved by Robinson? I can't say, and that's not really the issue, I suppose. What matters here is that Clemente *did* benefit from Robinson's crossing of the color line in baseball's modern era. It's a microcosm of how Latinos in football and baseball were aided by the strides made by African American players.

FLA: I'm thinking of those student protests at NYU in 1940–1941 that called for the end of racial discrimination in collegiate sports. Their chant "Bates Must Play" was a direct reaction to NYU Violet's coach's decision not to let him play alongside his white teammates in a game against University of Missouri Tigers. Some of the early protests against racial discrimination in the leagues that focused on the Black and White problem must have had an impact on Latinos, even if indirectly.

DOI: 10.1057/9781137403094

CG: I mentioned this event briefly a moment ago, and it was a direct result of the so-called gentleman's agreement between collegiate football teams. What those NYU students did, *in 1941*, has to be seen as nothing short of remarkable. Here you have students protesting that one of their fellow students, Bates, was not allowed to play on his own team simply because of *another* university's racist policies. Two decades later the sitting president of the United States had to send troops to desegregate the University of Alabama. Juxtaposing these two moments in American history reveals much about the geography of racism in the university system as well as the power of a socially conscious, highly motivated student body. University students have historically risen to the occasion—often putting themselves in harm's way—in order to protest the significant social injustices of their time. In turn, if students at NYU were denouncing the racist treatment of one of their own African American classmates, denouncing racist treatment *of all racial and ethnic groups* would certainly have been seen as an acceptable action to take against institutionalized racism. Because Latinos and African Americans are both minority groups that were treated with less-than status, these groups would have benefitted from the pursuit of equality in all arenas of American life, sport or otherwise.

FLA: It's certainly the case that with Latinos as neither Black nor White, it was easier for general managers, coaches—and team players—to discriminate against Latinos without people pointing fingers. Rather, during these earlier decades Latinos like those mentioned in our last chapter along with Californian Joe Hernández (1940–), Tejano Willie Crafts, and others, tended not to protest, but rather simply to slip across the border into the CFL as a backdoor (mostly but not always) into the U.S. pro teams. As A&M–Kingsville's star player you'd think that Crafts would be a first round draftee; everybody knew that he'd taken the team to their first national championship (1959). He was passed over. Instead, he crossed over into Canada and signed with the Edmonton Eskimos (1959–1960); later he crossed back over into the U.S. to play for the Denver Broncos, then coach back at A&M Kingsville.

CG: We have to remember that football players like any sport players, want to play. They don't simply want to be a member of a team. Latino football players, faced with the decision to wait and be drafted into the NFL and perhaps not play, often decided to seek playing opportunities north in the CFL. Crafts had to take the step that so many football

DOI: 10.1057/9781137403094

players have had to take in circumventing the NFL in order to get into the NFL. It's really another kind of test these players must pass, as if NFL organization and coaches require these players to go to Canada to "prove" they have the talent. While some players go to Canada to further hone their skills, Crafts was clearly one of the best players available when he became draft eligible.

FLA: Around the time in the 1950s when football had taken the lead over baseball as America's most popular sport (a way to smokescreen the shadow that covered the country during the draconian period of McCarthyism?), we began to see more Latinos drafted directly from college into NFL. We talked earlier about the GI Bill.

Athletic scholarships were also becoming more readily available. They weren't racially targeted scholarships, of course, but they did open the doors for talented players like Ray Romero from Wichita, Kansas, to get into the game. He realized that he could use his talent to get a scholarship to attend Kansas State University. Once there he honed his skills and went on to be drafted by the Philadelphia Eagles as their offensive guard...

CG: You bring up two key issues here, Frederick. The first is the rise of football's popularity, a position it would never relinquish. Its popularity coincided with the rise of television, and of course the money generating operation of football became a runaway train.

The second issue circles us back to the affordability of higher education. The GI Bill was crucial for so many students, but also the further expansion of athletic scholarships, which allowed many students from economically impoverished homes the opportunity to pursue education *and* athletic goals.

FLA: Athletic scholarships were the *way out* of poverty or working-class conditions for many Latinos during this period. I think here of two of the more famous players during this period. There was Tom Flores (1937–) who attended the College of the Pacific (after playing for Fresno City College and San Jose State) on a scholarship. And there was Joe Kapp (1938–) who won a basketball scholarship to attend UC Berkeley (Cal) but ended up playing football.

CG: Much different than the heydays of Yale and Harvard as football powerhouses, isn't it? Whereas early on only the sons of the wealthy played football, the athletic scholarship later allowed all students from

DOI: 10.1057/9781137403094

working-class families the opportunity to gain entrance into these institutions of higher learning via their athletic ability. That it was an athletic scholarship that gave Tom Flores the opportunity to further develop as a player, and later, as a coach, points to a significant turn in the development of professional athletes in the U.S. Flores is the most important Latino we've mentioned so far vis-à-vis professional football, and I'm sure we'll discuss him further. It also shows just how important an inclusive approach was for the development of Latinos in the NFL. Without the financial assistance Flores received via an athletic scholarship, he never would have had the opportunity to become the outstanding figure in the modernization of the NFL that he became. Incidentally, that he is not in the Pro Football Hall of Fame is simply outrageous. We must get to that issue before long.

FLA: In an important turn of events for Latinos in the NFL, Kapp decided to play football for Cal instead. His presence lifted the team to that of serious collegiate contender status.

CG: That *Sports Illustrated* cover from 1970 of Joe Kapp when he was with the Minnesota Vikings, emblazoned with the title "The Toughest Chicano," is an amazing thing to behold. It's also interesting to note that Kapp has been inducted into several major halls of fame, including the Canadian Football Hall of Fame, the Collegiate Football Hall of Fame, the UC Athletic Hall of Fame, but he is not in the Pro Football Hall of Fame. It may be that his NFL career simply wasn't long enough, but it does make one wonder why such a terrific football player spent seven years playing in Canada—essentially the years of his prime—before he played in the NFL.

FLA: Like other Latinos such as Crafts and Hernandez just mentioned, along with so many others, in spite of Flores's and Kapp's status as star college footballers—as a passer Flores ranked sixth and as offense fourth in the nation and Kapp single-handedly turned Cal into a serious contender—their careers were rerouted through the CFL. Both ended up playing for the Calgary Stampeders. While Flores injured his shoulder and returned to the U.S., Kapp ended up playing for the BC Lions (1961–1966).

CG: Exactly. It's frustrating to hear people wonder where the Latinos in the NFL were. My answer is that they were in Canada. Now, this always sounds like they must not have been "good enough" to make it in the

DOI: 10.1057/9781137403094

NFL, but that's simply preposterous. Flores and Kapp are prime examples. These are two of the great football players of all time, and their NFL playing careers were effectively shortened because they necessarily took their game to the CFL. Plus, it's not like they gave the NFL the early years of their careers—the best years. In fact, the opposite is true. You have to wonder what impelled players like Crafts, Hernández, Flores, and Kapp to play in Canada first. It cannot be that they didn't have the ability to play in the NFL. Their collegiate careers suggest otherwise.

FLA: In 1960 the Raiders picked up Flores as their first starting quarterback. And when Kapp returned to the U.S. he played for the Minnesota Vikings (1967–1969), taking the Vikings to the NFL Championship Game (1969). However, at least for Kapp his skills as a footballer didn't ultimately secure his future. Sidelined in the draft at the end of the 1969 season, he had to wait out a season before getting picked up by the Boston Patriots in 1970. And here's the kicker. When the Patriots signed him it was as a second-string quarterback and a four-year contract that made Kapp the highest paid player in the NFL.

Kapp possibly changed football history—for future Latinos and possibly all other minorities…

CG: I want to spend a bit more time on Flores before discussing Kapp further. As a quarterback with the Oakland Raiders, Flores became the first Latino quarterback in professional football history. The importance of this turn of events cannot be overstated. The quarterback position is seen as *the high-profile position*—the position that requires the greatest skill set of leadership and intelligence. When a team loses or wins, the quarterback is almost always the reason why. The quarterback touches the ball more than any other player on the field. He is truly second in leadership only to the head coach as far as the rest of the team is concerned. That Flores was given the helm as a quarterback was a huge breakthrough for Latinos in professional football. Remember that the quarterback position has historically been a locus for racial thinking in American sports (e.g., blacks aren't intelligent enough to play quarterback).

As for Kapp, he took what Flores had done to the next level. But as I mentioned, the NFL did not get Kapp's prime athletic years. His contract with the Patriots signaled that, even relatively late in his career, Kapp was one of the best at his position. He was the type of quarterback that was physical and didn't retreat from physical contact on the field. Kapp wasn't just riding the bench, he was shaping the position of quarterback

DOI: 10.1057/9781137403094

for many who would follow, and he was changing minds on what Latino football players could be in the game of professional football.

FLA: Of course, to this silver lining, we have to consider that Kapp like other players experienced his fair share of racial discrimination, including name-calling "Big Mex" or "Mexican Joe." And, his being dropped like a brick by the Patriots a year after he signed with them. The Patriots had drafted Plunkett, and when Kapp showed up for training, he was turned away. One too many Latinos for the Patriots…

CG: Joe Namath was called "Broadway Joe," and Joe Kapp was called "Mexican Joe." Seems fair, doesn't it? This continues the embarrassing tradition of giving race- and ethnicity-based nicknames to certain players. As for the Patriots, I'm sure it wasn't good to have two Latinos vying for the same position—the same *important* position—on its team. Perhaps if either Plunkett or Kapp had been a kicker, they could have both stayed on the team. But Kapp's unceremonious release from the Patriots was a sad end to Kapp's amazing playing career. He never played another down again. On the upside, Kapp was the head football coach at Cal during the famous 1982 Cal vs. Stanford game that ended on the final play, now famously remembered definitively as "The Play," with announcer Joe Starkey shrieking, "The band is out on the field!" Some have called it the greatest end of a football game ever.

FLA: Before we move on to Plunkett's story, I think it's important for us to remember that Kapp and other Latinos who were coming into their own as pro footballers during the 1960s lived during a time of great civil rights gains. The Bates protests at NYU in the early 1940s were small potatoes compared to the kind of civil rights mobilizations taking place around the country, pressuring administrations like that of the Kennedy presidency to dash the ground color lines in all aspects of everyday life—including football. There are many examples to talk about, including how the mistreatment of black footballers during their stay in New Orleans killed the AFL All-Star game in 1965.

CG: Sports have often been a site of social protest. Recall in the 1968 Olympic Games in Mexico City, Mexico the protest of Tommie Smith and John Carlos, who gave the Black Power salute as they received their Olympic medals, and were subsequently stripped of the medals they had earned. The 1965 AFL All-Star game highlighted two things: the continued pervasive nature of racism in the South, and the growing power of minority

DOI: 10.1057/9781137403094

athletes to rebuke the racist system. African American players couldn't even get a taxi in New Orleans, and the players, led by Carlton Gilchrist, moved forward with a boycott of New Orleans while refusing to play in the game as long as it was held in that city. The game was moved to Houston, Texas, and today few people may remember the outcome of the game in terms of who won and who lost. More importantly, the significant development of that event was the initiative demonstrated by the players. No longer were they going to take racist attitudes passively as many had done before them. It's an important drawing of the line in the sand, as it were.

FLA: I think too of how in 1961 the Kennedy Administration stamped down hard on Redskins (formerly the Boston Braves) owner George Preston Marshall to change his draft practices. The Redskins were the only pro football team *not* to have signed an African American. Marshall's answer: to hire a Native American, "Lone Star" Dietz, to coach the team. With a Native American as coach, no one could call out racism in their draft procedures. And, while blacks continued to be discriminated against, Dietz had drafted a Samoan, Hawaiian, American Indian, and Latino.

CG: And with a Native American as head coach, who could complain about the offensive nature of calling the team "Redskins"? But the writing was on the wall for Marshall, even if the Kennedy Administration had not applied pressure. All of the other NFL teams were drafting top-notch African American players, and since the NFL is in the business of winning (because winning typically equals higher revenues), the Redskins were going to be forced to draft black players, even if Marshall didn't want to. The external pressure only increased the inevitable.

FLA: Blacks and others of all walks of life boycotted and picketed the Redskins games.

CG: It's evidence of how intertwined sport is with the social pulse of the nation. That's why I don't understand how many scholars in the humanities take little interest in what happens in sports. I argue that we can't fully understand things like racism without looking critically at American sports. Whether sports lags behind social progress or is at the head of the curve, it's always of significance.

FLA: In an odd twist to the story, because of the negative publicity brought on by the boycotts and picketing of stadiums, when Dietz did draft a Black player in 1962, it was Jose "Joe" M. Hernández (1940–)—an Afrolatino from Arizona whose career also had to take the Canada route

DOI: 10.1057/9781137403094

(Edmonton Eskimos in 1963 and 1966–1970) before becoming *eligible* to play in the U.S. leagues.

Whether this was a deliberate move to skirt pressure to bring blacks onto the team or not, the fact is in this surprising twist to the story, they drafted a Latino.

CG: I'm not sure if the drafting of Hernández was a sort of slap in the face of protesters or whether it was just an odd twist, but it does complicate the often-simplified Black vs. White binary when people think of race, particularly in sports. And we have the Canadian connection in play here once more.

FLA: The Washington Redskins discriminated against blacks yet ended up having one of the strongest track records for drafting Latinos of all the teams in the NFL…

CG: Many of the Latinos we've already discussed were first drafted by Washington—Flores and Kapp, for instance. But when you dig deeper, there is something curious going on. Washington was drafting Latinos, but they often did nothing more with those players than draft them, which is why they often left to play in Canada. It makes me wonder if it wasn't another maneuver by the organization to save face or to deflect criticism of entrenched racist attitudes held by management.

FLA: Another team that had a consistently strong record for recruiting Latinos was Oakland; and it didn't have the same xenophobic policies in other areas of the draft. We'll talk about Tom Flores in a minute, but already in 1962 the Raiders also drafted the LA born and raised defensive back, Henry "Hank" Rivera (1938–1996). He helped them turn their game around from a series of losses to an important victory over the Boston Patriots. And, this same year they drafted José Hernandez (1962) and Chon Gallegos (1939–) as their back up quarterback to Cotton Davidson as well as Vernon Valdez as defensive back and quarterback. In 1963 the Raiders also lassoed Herman "Squirming Herman" Urenda from the College of Pacific; like Ray Romero and Tom Flores, he was also on scholarship. But, like Vernon and others playing during this period, he was drafted and served in the military during the Korean War.

CG: Unlike the Washington Redskins, Latino players who were drafted by Oakland actually saw significant playing time. It also makes me think of the reputation Oakland established early on as a team that didn't always do what other teams did. Thanks in large part to the team's

DOI: 10.1057/9781137403094

independent-minded owner Al Davis, the Raiders fashioned an image of the rebel who did things with the spirit of independent panache. If we are quick to lay blame at the feet of George Preston Mitchell for not drafting black players, we need to heap great praise on Al Davis for his open-mindedness in a time when it was not popular to be so freethinking.

FLA: While all the teams passed over Gallegos in the draft—his 5'9", 170 pound stature didn't inspire confidence – the Raiders asked him to come to their training camp for a tryout. He made the team and signed as a free agent with the Raiders.

CG: It really is an unheard of thing to allow a player of Gallegos's stature to play quarterback. Think of Doug Flutie constantly being told that he was too short to play quarterback, and he's an inch taller than Gallegos! Again, I think this speaks of the innovative thinking that characterizes the Oakland Raiders at this time. A few years ago this might have been called "outside the box" thinking, but it's simply a situation where the organization resisted categorizing or stereotyping certain players, and instead, allowed the player to show how they could best allow the team to succeed. Famously, Al Davis's mantra for the Raiders has been and continues to be, "Just win, baby!" He was an owner who wasn't going to let his eyes be deceived by social constructions of inequality. That's not to say Davis was a civil rights leader or anything like that. But he above all other owners never allowed issues of race, ethnicity, or stereotypes cloud his judgment on what the team needed in order to win. Not only did Davis draft minority players at greater numbers compared to other teams, he was the first to implement a starting Latino quarterback (Flores), the first to hire a Latino head coach (Flores), and one of first to hire an African American coach (Art Shell).

FLA: Christopher, might we say that the arrival on the pro football scene first of Tom Flores then Jim Plunkett (1947–) marked a massive watershed moment for Latinos in the NFL.

CG: I think both of these men can be credited with really giving Latinos a stake in the NFL game. Flores was quite a significant player, and he was an even greater head coach in the NFL. Not only did he take the reigns after John Madden's retirement from coaching, Flores also became an important mentor for many players, such as Marcus Allen and Jim

DOI: 10.1057/9781137403094

Plunkett. He also shaped many coaches who would follow after him, such as Art Shell.

But Jim Plunkett really marks the moment a Latino was drafted by an NFL team and was expected to become a leader on the team. Plunkett did not have to circumvent the NFL by going to Canada; he was the overall number one pick. He was blessed with immense football talent, and he happened to come from a working-class Chicano family in California. Plunkett is my first memory of a Chicano in the NFL; my mother insisted that I knew of Plunkett's heritage, even if his surname didn't sound like it was akin to my own. Though I became aware of Plunkett in the twilight of his career, I was old enough to watch on television as he won the Super Bowl against the Washington Redskins on January 22, 1984. (I was in the third grade, and it's the first Super Bowl I remember watching in its entirety.) And while Plunkett's coach had the last name of Flores, I was blissfully ignorant of the watershed moment in the NFL that I had just witnessed. As an eight year old, I had no reason to think there couldn't be more Jim Plunketts and Tom Floreses in the NFL. So, to your question, Frederick, we might take it even a step further and recall that Super Bowl XVIII, which featured a Latino head coach and Latino starting quarterback on the winning team *for the second time*, has not happened since. Thus for me, that Super Bowl in 1984 is unquestionably *the* defining moment for Latinos in the NFL. Flores and Plunkett had won the Super Bowl a few years earlier, but a second win could not be dismissed as luck. Nothing has come close to beating it since.

FLA: Both Flores and Plunkett hail from pretty modest backgrounds. Flores grew up in and around Fresno; when not in school and playing football he was picking in the fields alongside his parents. Plunkett grew up in and around San Jose working odd jobs to help his progressively blind father and already blind mother support the family. At James Lick High School in San Jose, Plunkett's superheroic capacity to throw the football came to the attention of Chon Gallegos who had since left the Raiders to coach the high school football team. For both Flores and Plunkett, football wasn't so much a way out (at least in their early years) as it was *a way of survival....*

CG: It was another way to channel their strong work ethic. Flores has talked about how he likes to see himself not as a Latino who works hard, but rather as someone who works hard and happens to be Latino. In other words, his sense of Latinidad does not define him, but it does

DOI: 10.1057/9781137403094

happen to play a significant role in why he has such a determined work ethic. Funny how it plays opposite to the stereotypically "lazy" Mexican that television and film popularized in the early to middle 20th century. These two Latino men were incredibly gifted with exceptional physical abilities, and, we might add, intelligence. But what allowed them to stand out were the opportunities to use their physical gifts for more than just manual labor. They must have recognized early on that they had the physical gifts for playing football at a high level, and they happened to be born in a time and place where the necessary resources were within reach.

FLA: It wasn't as a football player that gave Flores a special place in Latino football history. Rather, it was the moment in 1979 when Flores replaced John Madden as *head coach*. He was the first Latino ever to be placed in such a position in the NFL. Flores took the Raiders to the Super Bowl XV in 1981 with a 27–10 triumph over the Philadelphia Eagles.

CG: True, though as I mentioned before, Flores was the first Latino to start at quarterback in professional football when he played with the Raiders. Technically, he's not the first Latino to start at quarterback in the NFL because, at the time, the Raiders were a part of the AFL. But it was professional football nonetheless. However, his successes as a head coach in the NFL do outshine his achievements as a player. Flores coached the Raiders to a Super Bowl victory not once, but *twice*. And yet, for all of his achievements, he still has not been inducted into the Pro Football Hall of Fame. It's a disgrace.

FLA: We tend to think about individuals leading teams to victory, Christopher. But of course there were all the team members working with Flores that brought the Raiders to victory. Of these team members there was the other Latino, Jim Plunkett, who played a significant role in this Super Bowl victory—and not by design. Quarterback Dan Pastorini's injury pulled Plunkett off the bench and lead the Raider offense...

CG: It was like destiny. I couldn't help recall my memories of that particular Super Bowl a moment ago. I now realize that it was the moment I became a fan of the NFL, and it's striking that it should be so special for having had two Latinos in key positions in the game for the second time. It's a game that truly belongs to the ages. There may have been other Super Bowls that were more exciting or dynamic— the Raiders were pretty much in control for much of the game—but

DOI: 10.1057/9781137403094

there have been few Super Bowls as significant in terms of minority representation. This was no fluke. Perhaps the Washington Redskin's victory over the Denver Broncos in 1988 is as significant for having had Doug Williams, an African American, quarterback his team to a resounding victory. It was the first time an African American had started in a Super Bowl.

FLA: Plunkett secured an MVP for taking the Raiders to victory at the Super Bowl XV and he took the Raiders to a championship victory in Super Bowl XVIII. Yet, he has yet to be inducted into the Pro Football Hall of Fame.

CG: Issues of identity aside, Plunkett should have been a first-ballot Hall of Famer. What I mean by that is he should have been inducted after the mandatory five-years-after-retirement mark and not a day more. Consider John Elway, whose record in Super Bowls is 2–3. Despite losing three Super Bowls, he was inducted into the Hall of Fame in his first year of eligibility. Both Plunkett and Elway were drafted out of Stanford. Plunkett won the Heisman Trophy and Elway did not. Both won exactly two Super Bowls, and Elway is the one that has his bust in Canton. I'm not saying Elway isn't deserving, but Plunkett is the *only* two time winning Super Bowl quarterback that is *not* in the Pro Football Hall of Fame. Just think of what Tom Flores and Jim Plunkett achieved in professional football, then entertain the idea that they're somehow not good enough to be inducted with the best that ever played the game. The NFL and the Pro Football Hall of Fame cannot be taken seriously if they continue to neglect recognizing these two men: The only Latino to win two Super Bowls as a head coach (Flores); the only Latino to win the Super Bowl MVP (Plunkett). I mean, their exclusion would be a joke if it weren't a sad reality. The only way the NFL can come close to addressing this "oversight" is to induct them at the same time, and as soon as possible.

FLA: Might we say that the Pro Football Hall of Fame has a history of being racist? There are of course those Black star footballer we've mentioned such as Frederick "Fritz" Pollard as well as others we haven't mentioned like Charles W. Follis and Joe Lilliard that made history crossing the color line but have yet to be recognized. What about Kapp, Joe Arenas who was one of the best kickers of his generation, Flores or Plunkett, the only quarterback to start and win two Super Bowls, or any number of recent remarkable Latino players.

DOI: 10.1057/9781137403094

CG: A few thoughts come to mind. I wonder if more Latinos would already be inducted if there were more former players who voted on deserving nominees. The Selection Committee of the Pro Football Hall of Fame must bear the responsibility for deserving players they have, for whatever reason, decided to ignore. I could imagine arguments being made against some of the players you listed above, but if Tom Flores and Jim Plunkett don't have the necessary *bona fides* to be inducted, then the Pro Football Hall of Fame must be viewed as a sham. I don't know if it's racist thinking, or whether the committee is somehow disregarding or diminishing the accomplishments of many of the Latinos you mentioned, but the omissions speak volumes as to what the Selection Committee, and ultimately the NFL, values. For example, there are only three kickers inducted (George Blanda, Jan Stenerud, and Lou Groza), and is it simply a coincidence that Latinos have historically been kickers more often than any other position? I mean, all one has to do is look at the facts and draw immediate conclusions. Something is certainly not right in Canton. And as long as Flores and Plunkett remain waiting outside the Pro Football Hall of Fame, it's probably best to think of it as the Pro Football "Hall of Fame."

FLA: African American players struggled, but Latinos were out rightly excluded? Or was this chicken/egg: Latinos not playing football at school or in playground (baseball and soccer instead) so none are out there to recruit?

CG: I feel it is a mixture of both. There may have been fewer Latinos to recruit due to cultural factors (familial obligations that precluded pursuing higher education) and accessibility issues (harder to get quality primary and secondary school education, making it harder to enter college). But there were clearly other factors that made it easy to ignore and exclude Latino football players. Or, if they were brought on to the team, it didn't equate to actually participating as a full-fledged member of the team. One final issue to consider is the lack of Latinos in the NFL to inspire younger generations and also to educate those whose narrow minded thinking seeks to limit what Latinos are capable of. Plunkett and Flores inspired me, not to become a quarterback or coach, per se, but to reassure me that my physical talents could be used for more than clipping onions or picking oranges.

FLA: In reflecting on the stories we have weaved together into this elaborate tapestry, I ask: How much of Latino football history during this

DOI: 10.1057/9781137403094

period of the brown color line is made by happenstance or strategy—or both.

CG: I feel that the barriers Latinos have encountered throughout football history are more often than not strategic. Conversely, I've no doubt that the advances of and successes by Latinos in football are aided by happenstance. I don't mean that Latinos were lucky or were given accolades when they didn't deserve it. In fact, as the continued exclusion of Kapp, Flores, and Plunkett from the Pro Football Hall of Fame shows, Latinos are often given their due only begrudgingly, even when they have worked through the most difficult of circumstances to achieve their successes. But for being in the right place at the right time, we may have never had a Kapp, a Flores, and Plunkett in the NFL. In turn this begs the question, how many Latinos who had the physical attributes to be success stories in the NFL just happened to be in the wrong place at the wrong time? Until Latinos and other minority groups have the same level of accessibility as whites, and until Latinos and other minority groups are given the same sorts of praise for their achievements as whites, the game of professional football will need to continue to be shaped from without and within by those who are determined to stamp out such unequal opportunities that exist in America's premiere sport.

DOI: 10.1057/9781137403094

3

Sidelined...*No Más!*

Abstract: *"Sidelined...No Más!"* considers issues of access
to education (GI Bill, athletic scholarships, and Affirmative
Action), the increased diversification in the regional and
heritage of Latino players (from urban to rural and from
Mexican to Puerto Rican to Dominican and Cuban of origin),
and the presence of Latinos in the globalization of the game.

Frederick Luis Aldama and Christopher González. *Latinos
in the End Zone: Conversations on the Brown Color Line in
the NFL.* New York: Palgrave Macmillan, 2014.
DOI: 10.1057/9781137403094.

Frederick Luis Aldama: Since the late 20th century our numbers as Latinos in the U.S. have been growing exponentially. As we both know just by stepping outside our front doors, Christopher, we are everywhere. Today, we are the largest minority in the U.S. Already in 2010 we numbered upwards of 51 million (not including the 12 million-plus that are undocumented)...

Christopher González: It is an interesting situation in the U.S. right now, and as a Latino, I find it particularly fascinating. But you and I are not the only ones who have noticed this significant continuing uptick in the number of Latinos. While politics is still trying to grapple with the issue of undocumented Latinos and the subject of immigration, businesses and enterprises don't necessarily wait for the law of the land to catch up to the realities of what people like you and I see when taking a stroll through town. Not only is the number of Latinos rising, the purchasing power of those Latinos is also rising. Suddenly Latinos are an important market for businesses, and Latinos themselves are becoming creators, not just consumers, of business.

FLA: For a long time we as Latinos lived and worked in rural, agricultural areas of the U.S. This was where the work was for many of our families. After World War II the Latino population increased ever more and settled mainly in large towns and cities, where their economic life shifted from agriculture to factory production and consumer industries. This shift brought about new lifestyles and new worldviews—and in some instances, more time for the next generation to pursue what we might consider to be extraneous activities like sports; extra in the sense that they don't have an immediate economic return that might help put food on a family's table, for instance. With this urbanization came the exposure to all variety of different possible ways of realizing one's potentialities, whether in sports or elsewhere.

To clarify this more, let me turn to a contemporary result of this Latino urbanization: Mark (Travis John) Sanchez as the Latino quarterback for the New York Jets—a figure that will come up again later in our conversation. Sanchez is a third-generation U.S. born Latino who came of age as a football player during a time when it seemed possible for a Latino to be a quarterback. Recall those early periods we discussed when Latinos weren't even considered viable athletes in football with many crossing the border into Canada to *prove* themselves to the NFL. Growing up in Orange County area of greater Los Angeles, Sanchez is very much the

DOI: 10.1057/9781137403094

product of an urban existence that moved from blue-collar roots (his father was a fire captain) into the professional classes. He became a quarterback in the NFL and not, say, a farmer in the California Central Valley.

CG: Mark Sanchez, and even Jim Plunkett before him, exemplifies something I attempted to articulate in the last chapter—that early on Latinos with the potential to play professional football needed to have so many opportunities line up perfectly in order to make their dream a reality. Mark Sanchez, because he was born in a specific situation within a historic time period conducive for Latino success in professional football, necessarily makes us hearken back to years past when Latino families *didn't* have the sort of economic flexibility or educational resources to make it through the pipeline to the NFL.

If we take the two issues together, the rising number of Latinos with upward social mobility and economic might, coupled with a greater proliferation of Latinos in all walks of American life (not simply the *labores* where migrant workers make their living), we should anticipate many more Latinos in the NFL, and not just as kickers. We'll begin to see them not as exceptions to the rule, but as a very normalized expectation for what we find in NFL players.

FLA: This isn't to say that our demographic numbers and urbanization are a cure all. While we see more Sanchezes in the NFL than we did Kapps in his era, Latinos still face huge obstacles, starting with all sorts of problems that shadow Latino kids in our public education system. We have many a Latino kid who dreams of becoming a football player—or a professor, doctor, artist, and more, but they are still falling through the rips of an increasingly shredded social tissue.

CG: That's true. Greater numbers won't necessarily translate to more Latino professors or NFL players. Just because more Latino families are what we call white-collar, we shouldn't fall into the trap of believing that Latino families still do not encounter significant barriers in American society. For instance, in the midst of President Barack Obama's presidency I continue to hear people argue that the first African American president in U.S. history somehow equates to a situation where the African American community no longer faces problems such as, for example, racism. Obama's election (and re-election) is undoubtedly one of the high watermarks in America's history with race, but his election doesn't suddenly wipe clean such things as institutionalized prejudice and racism.

DOI: 10.1057/9781137403094

Similarly, Tom Flores and Jim Plunkett, while smashing the Brown Color Line in the NFL like no one before or since, weren't able to single-handedly remove all barriers for potential Latino football players. Those barriers still exist in some form or another. And not all of the barriers are situated within, say, the education system. It has been a struggle for Latino families to see something like sports as valuable and not simply as playtime that will take away precious resources from the family. More and more Latino families, particularly of those in the third generation or later, are more apt to encourage their children to pursue higher education or collegiate/professional sports than more recently arrived generations. This is generally speaking, of course; there are exceptions to this trend.

FLA: Of course, a fundamental and foundational ingredient in the healthy growth of children is their physical education. In fact, the education of our body to move in the world in carefully orchestrated ways is inseparable from our intellectual and emotional education.

CG: You have to be taught how to dribble a basketball. And if you ever want the kind of basketball "handles" on display with some of the great point guards in the NBA, you need the opportunity to develop those skills. I can remember receiving a "U" for unsatisfactory on my kindergarten report card because I could not dribble a ball yet. I delighted in other forms of physical play—playing tag, throwing a football, kicking a ball—but I had not had the opportunity to learn how to dribble a basketball at that age. Though I never played organized basketball outside of pick up games with my brothers or friends, I still cannot dribble well with my non-dominant hand. Perhaps I missed a critical learning period for dribbling well with either hand.

My point here is to reinforce what you're saying, but also to underscore the idea that children need the opportunity to learn these athletic skills. Plus, there is also an element of self-esteem that goes along with this issue. People may see certain children who haven't had the chance to develop some of these physical abilities, such as hand-eye coordination, as clumsy. Worse, the child may see him- or herself as clumsy. Clumsiness, of course, is often equated with buffoonery and an untidy intellect. So there is no question that children need opportunities to explore their physical abilities and talents, and early on. My caveat, however, is that children also need the freedom to develop these skills from the high-pressure stakes of winning at all costs. There will be plenty of time for

DOI: 10.1057/9781137403094

that when the child's self-esteem and fortitude are mature enough to handle it. So, risk free athletic development as a young child is the way to go. And that's not just my opinion; that's the general consensus in child development and sports psychology research.

FLA: Yet, we find that today an increasing majority of children no longer even have physical education offered at their schools. Of course, because of the way race and class are knotted together, this means that these are the schools where the greatest number of Latino kids attend.

CG: It's sad that so many states want to squeeze every bit out of a child's intellect but completely neglect the child's physical development. And it's not just physical education, though that is the most recent area of a student's educational experience that is seen as expendable. Music and art have also come under fire in the last 10–15 years. I don't want to derail our focus here, but the issue of standardization of education—and specifically high-stakes testing—is at the root of all this.

In my home state of Texas, students have their first high-pressure test in the third grade. Many students, after an entire day at school, stay after school for exam-specific tutoring. A student's entire school career funnels him or her to the high-stakes test. And if a school can devote more time to a student's ability to perform well on one of these tests, be it by reducing the amount of time for lunch, eliminating play and physical education, doing away with music and art, then the school will do it. Nationwide, billions of dollars hinge on the status of schools, which is determined in large measure by how their students perform on the high-stakes test.

FLA: As we already discussed, the GI Bill and athletic scholarships played a crucial role for footballers like Kapp, Romero, Flores. However, the real strides forward came after the 1960s civil rights struggles and victories when the lower and higher public education system in this country was forced to *include* rather than continue on its path to exclude.

CG: I mentioned the issue of segregation in the previous chapters, and to my mind that's a significant moment where we can say a social policy directly impacted the sports world. For too long Jim Crow had been the law of the land in both society at large and the world of sports. Once all schools were forced to desegregate, high school and collegiate sports would be forced to open up as well. It's not happenstance that

DOI: 10.1057/9781137403094

professional football began to be much more inclusive by the mid- to late-1960s. And the first Super Bowl was held in 1970, in the wake of the civil rights movements spurred on by many minority groups in the country.

FLA: Might we dare to tread into the zone of Affirmative Action? I hear the argument constantly that Latino college athletes got into the Ohio State University or any number of other colleges because of their athletic ability, and not their smarts.

CG: We'd be remiss if we didn't raise the issue of Affirmative Action. It's such a crucial and controversial issue in American life from the late 20th century to the present, and it impacts higher education as well as the world of professional sports. Unfortunately I'm sure there are some athletes, Latino or otherwise, who got into high profile programs more on their athletic ability rather than their test scores. To me, though, that's not an issue of Affirmative Action. All athletic programs want the best athletes they can muster with the available scholarship funds at hand, and the most elite programs aren't necessarily interested in how high a recruit's SAT score might be. Academic issues only become an issue when the student is not at the minimum standard for, say, eligibility purposes. Affirmative Action comes up in the arena of university admissions at large, which in its own right is an area for further debate, as the courts continually reveal. In terms of athletic programs, Affirmative Action policies ensured that programs did not exclude potential recruits solely based on race or ethnicity. But these athletes from underrepresented groups are not being given starting positions on the teams of elite programs in order to check a box. Today these programs want to win, unlike in decades past when universities and teams adhered to exclusionary practices even at the detriment of their own success.

FLA: One of the most brilliant of our contemporary authors, John Edgar Wideman, is the product of college athletic Affirmative Action policies. And, I wouldn't be writing this book with you, Christopher, as a professor at a top-shelf university if it weren't for Affirmative Action policies still in play at UC Berkeley in the late 1980s...

CG: True, but Frederick Luis Aldama and John Edgar Wideman were not simply given things that they didn't earn. The Affirmative Action policies allowed you, Frederick, and Wideman a way into traditionally exclusionary institutions of higher education where you both were

DOI: 10.1057/9781137403094

allowed to develop your innate abilities and talents. Affirmative Action has been and continues to be at the center of political debate, and that's not going to end anytime soon. You'll find people for or against it in nearly every demographic you can devise. But no one can deny that this proactive policy destroyed the locks on the gates of the ivory towers of academia and, if I may expand my metaphor, continues to allow people, regardless of group affiliation, entrance into the waiting room where they might be considered for admittance. It frustrates me to hear how those who have achieved great success during the time of Affirmative Action somehow indicates they were given something they didn't truly earn. The Affirmative Action policy didn't write Wideman's books. It didn't write the many scholarly books of Aldama. Critiquing the policy is fair game. But a person who wants to denigrate someone's achievements because they come from an underrepresented group in the time of Affirmative Action isn't worthy of a serious debate.

FLA: So perhaps we should consider the "Browning of America" as at once a step forward (we are seeing more Latinos in pro football), but with some inching backward too. While there's certainly been a blitz in terms of Latinos playing in the NFL—and all variety of positions—but at other levels we're still way behind. I can count on one hand the number of Latinos who've been placed in coaching positions in the entire history of the NFL: Tom Fears, Tom Flores, and Honduran-born assistant coach Steve Van Buren.

Even today we can look at the demographic make up of Division I coaches and see a problem. There's certainly been an uptick since the bad old days of the color line, but it's still not a level playing field by any means. In 2009 we had nine Division I coaches that were of color: seven were black, one was Polynesian, and one was Latino. Certainly, this is nine more than the zero we had in the earlier years of the game. However, we have to keep in mind that these nine are but a drop in the bucket to the 100-plus white Division I coaches.

CG: There are a few important issues knocking about in what you just said. We must hold to the idea that *some* progress is not necessarily *sufficient* progress. As you say, nine is more than zero, but nine is not enough. Further, by and large head coaches were players at one time. One can think of the players as a potential pool from where future coaches will be selected. There are exceptions to this trend; take, for instance, Eric Mangini, who made his way through the coaching ranks from ball boy

DOI: 10.1057/9781137403094

on the Cleveland Browns squad coached by Bill Belichick to head football coach of the New York Jets. But my point here is that if there aren't many Latinos in the pool of players, there will be even fewer of those Latinos who will go on to become head coaches in the NFL. Currently there is only one Latino in a head coaching position in the NFL, and that is Ron Rivera of the Carolina Panthers. A record-breaking collegiate player when he was at Cal, Rivera was a standout linebacker for the Super Bowl winning Chicago Bears of 1985. His Puerto Rican heritage makes him the first Puerto Rican player to play on a winning Super Bowl team. He is generally very well respected as a coach—first as a defensive coordinator for the Bears, and now as head coach of the Panthers. So, if we include Rivera with the other Latino head football coaches in the NFL's history, we still can count them all on one hand.

It's easy to think of the paucity of Latino head coaches if we think of it as similar to Latinos with PhDs. If the pool of Latinos with undergraduate degrees is small, there will be fewer numbers of Latinos who enter grad school by default because not all undergraduates (of any group) will pursue a grad degree. The way to get more Latino PhDs is to increase grad school enrollment for Latinos. And in order to do that, you need to increase enrollment of Latinos as undergrads. It's almost the exact process for Latinos in the NFL.

One final issue here is something I referenced in an earlier chapter, the so-called Rooney Rule in the NFL. The rule is named after the long time owner of the Pittsburgh Steelers, Dan Rooney, who took the initiative to begin hiring minorities, particularly African Americans, in positions of leadership within his organization. The Rooney Rule is a type of self-imposed Affirmative Action on the part of the NFL, which states that an organization must interview a minority candidate when considering filling a head coaching or upper-level coaching position. It has received mixed reviews, and it may be more PR than anything else on the part of the NFL. Regardless, it does bring deserving minority candidates into the conversation and into the public consciousness if nothing else.

FLA: And, we are gravely underrepresented in other important areas like calling the shots as a referee. In 2010 we had the first Latino referee in the NFL, the Cuban-born émigré (part of the Peter Pan generation of the mid-1960s), Alberto Riveron.

The lack of Latino refs in the NFL could be a question of economics. Christopher, maybe you would know better the pipeline here, but it might be that Latinos aren't that interested because of the pennies it brings in.

DOI: 10.1057/9781137403094

I'm assuming you'd have to have another source of income (maybe even retired with a pension) to take this on. After all, as one Latino out of 120 refs in the NFL and as crew chief, Alberto Riveron would likely bring in something like $2,500 to $8,400 per game.

CG: You bring up a really important issue here, Frederick. There has been talk about having the NFL cadre of referees as being permanent employees of the NFL. In other words, there has been pressure on the NFL to hire referees who are career referees. As it stands now, NFL referees actually have full-time jobs in some other area. For example, one of the more prominent and respected NFL referees working today, Ed Hochuli, is a trial lawyer in Arizona. It's amazing that such an important figure in the multi-billion dollar a year game of professional football is hired as a part timer. We saw just how important the officials were at the start of the 2012 season when the first three weeks of games were officiated by well meaning but ultimately incapable replacement officials because of the lockout. Now, because of collective bargaining, NFL referees make more than Riveron did, roughly $10,000 per game, which sounds like a lot of money. But when you consider what the NFL profits per game, and understand how important the officials' jobs are, the compensation ought to be closer to what coaches and players make, in my opinion.

In terms of Latinos as NFL officials, I think it's again related to participation in the game. Hochuli, for instance, played collegiate football at UTEP, and thus had a keen interest in the game. His skills as an attorney make him an ideal person for the job of NFL referee. But based on the rising numbers of the Latino population you noted in the opening of this chapter, why wouldn't we expect the number of Latino NFL officials to uptick as well?

FLA: Riveron's recently become the league's Senior Director of Officiating. Maybe having a Latino helm the ship will change the ethnic landscape of those calling the shots from the sidelines.

CG: I think more than anything, having Latinos such as Riveron, and Ron Rivera, in important positions within the leadership and management side of the game of professional football can have its own positive effect in opening the doors for Latinos to come through. Whether or not Latinos like Riveron and Rivera realize it, just by being who they are, they are making it possible for other Latinos to take on the same sorts of responsibilities. And the more Latinos who enter these specific areas

DOI: 10.1057/9781137403094

in the NFL, the more Latinos we ought to expect to pursue careers in coaching and officiating, and management as well.

FLA: As we grow our Latino presence in the NFL diversity off the field will become increasingly important. I'm thinking of issues of trust between officials and players but also brown bodies in the stadium that function as a kind of superglue that holds it all together . . .

CG: The cumulative effect of what you just mentioned—the superglue— makes manifest Latinos' claim to the game of professional football. When Latinos are on the field in pads, on the sidelines with a coach's headset, in the black and white uniforms of the officials, and the fans both in the stadium and at home in front of the television, it creates what we simply might call presence. And there is a sense of ownership and belonging that goes along with that. For too long Latinos have been on the outside looking in when it comes to the NFL. But slowly we're beginning to see Latinos in all facets of the game. Better still, our presence is now raising fewer and fewer eyebrows. I can't stress enough just how importance that is.

FLA: Perhaps we should return to the issue of economics, not at the player end of things (we know they sign some hefty numbers) nor at the coach side (it wouldn't be difficult to scrape a living on their salaries), but at the level of those Latinos who go to the games, those who want to go to the games but can't afford it, and those who watch the games.

CG: The price of attending professional sports really is cost prohibitive, especially if we're talking about a family of four or five. It costs upwards of hundreds of dollars just to attend one NFL football game. Fortunately for football, it's a sport that translates very well through the medium of television. Watching the game at home with family and friends is a rewarding experience in and of itself. Consider that only a fraction of those who watch the Super Bowl every year actually attend the game. The celebration of the Super Bowl has become one of the premiere cultural events of the late 20th century, and it is done mostly as a social event in front of a television with plenty of food and drink to enjoy all the while. So, while the cost of attending a game may not be feasible, football is very much a social event that can be enjoyed without actually being at the game. No other sport can make this boast. People don't gather to watch 82 games in an NBA season, or 162 games in an MLB season. But a 16 game NFL season certainly works well as a social event.

DOI: 10.1057/9781137403094

FLA: If we set aside the deep problems in our education system that plague Latinos from the get-go, it seems clear that not having a Latino presence in and around the field is a case of bad economics. If white coaches and white referees are hiring those that look like them instead of talented Latinos who are the fastest growing population in the U.S., don't they risk alienating potential football goers (ticket sales) and TV audiences (merchandise and all other revenue streams that spin from the ads)?

CG: I think businesses in America are beginning to take notice. For the last few years the NFL has marketed itself heavily during Hispanic Heritage Month every September. NBC's "Sunday Night Football" broadcast has a gimmick where, during the broadcast, they call the teams by their Spanish designations (e.g., Los Vaqueros de Dallas) and allow the Spanish language play-by-play to be piped in for a play or two. Again, it's gimmicky, but it is a clear indication that the NFL understands where the market is growing. And these sorts of overtures to Latino audiences are only going to become a more significant aspect of the NFL game so long as the Latino population and its purchasing power continue to increase.

FLA: We've spent time weaving the different threads together of the earlier epoch of Latinos in the NFL, now let's take a look at the trends in our contemporary moment. While still relatively few compared to their White counterparts, Latinos are popping up all over field, from QB to linemen to receiver.

CG: More and more we are seeing Latinos take the NFL field in a variety of positions. It is certainly a terrific thing to see.

FLA: I wonder why we're still seeing the majority of Latinos as kickers. It seems that even those who are brought on for other positions end up as kickers.

CG: Beyond what I've said in earlier chapters, I really have no explanation for this phenomenon. Many of the Latinos who ultimately became kickers in the NFL were adept at soccer, but it truly does seem like an inordinate amount of Latinos in the position of kicker.

FLA: And, of course, unless you're a real aficionado people don't really know the kickers. They're never in the limelight. Might we consider them a bit like the janitors of the field...

DOI: 10.1057/9781137403094

CG: One only needs to look at how many kickers are in the Pro Football Hall of Fame. The kickers tend to be a unique position in the entire game of football. It is the one position where the play is about as scripted as it can be. The ball is stationary, angled by the holder in just the right way, and unless there is a problem that occurs between the moment the long snapper snaps the ball and the holder positions the ball, the kicker has no real variables that come into play. Think of similar instances in other sports. It's like a free throw in basketball or hitting a golf ball. Because one can practice kicking footballs in solitude, the dynamics for a kicker are much different than for nearly any other position. They don't need to practice in the same sorts of ways as other positions on the field. Kickers are specialists, but they are necessary. They can certainly make or break a game, and so they are crucial. But, like the quarterback, the kicker often receives an inordinate amount of blame or credit for a team's win. So, they are in the limelight in certain situations, but all one has to do is watch how the rest of the team treats a kicker when a crucial kick is imminent. He is left alone, and no one dares distract or reassure him. In a few moments, the kicker will either be riding on the shoulders of victory or will be taking the lonely walk of defeat.

FLA: Yet you and I know that Latino kickers have made games and put championship victories in pockets. I think off the cuff of those like: Guadalajara-born and LA-raised, Efrén Herrera (1951) as the kicker in Cowboy's Super Bowl XII victory (1978); Mexican pro-soccer player-cum-Cowboys-kicker, Rafael Septién (1978–1986); New Mexican Danny Villanueva who also took his skills (he played soccer for the American Youth Soccer Organization) to the Cowboys (1965–1967); Argentine-born, Florida-raised Martín Gramática who brought his kicking skills to the Tampa Bay Buccaneers for four seasons, making the All Pro team in 2000; seemingly in the blood, his brothers Bill and Santiago also kicked for teams like the Giants, Dolphins, among others; and there are significant Tejanos like Leo Araguz who proved an important piece in the puzzle for the Raiders (1996–2000), Vikings (2003), Seahawks (2005), and Ravens (2006). This is to name but a few of those invisible Latinos (we don't see them asked to strike poses for *GQ*, right?) whose skill on the field can *make and break* games.

CG: Exactly right. There is a certain invisibility of kickers that goes hand in hand with the invisibility of Latinos in the NFL's history. We only notice the kickers—Latino or otherwise—when they either win or lose

DOI: 10.1057/9781137403094

the game, or if they do something out of the ordinary, such as when Bill Gramática injured his kicking leg *after celebrating* a successful kick with the Arizona Cardinals.

FLA: A certain amount of speculation is involved here, but I can't help but think that there's still some deep sense from the top down (management to coaches) that sees brown bodies not as strategists, throwers, agile runners with sticky hands...but as cleats and a soccer ball.

CG: I think that's slowly beginning to change, but it cannot be mere coincidence that the most unobtrusive position in the game is where you find the majority of Latinos who've played the game.

FLA: You can speak directly to this, Christopher. I'm not sure your exact height and weight, but you're big fellow. Yet, there's this perception—*misperception*—that Latinos only come in small packages—as *chicaspatas*, to use the proverbial Mexican phrase.

CG: At the moment I'm 6 ft 2 in, 235 pounds. I have an older brother who is 6 ft 5 in, 285 pounds, though he competed as an athlete while over 315 pounds. And I have cousins who are even bigger. Apparently there was one great uncle in my family who was close to 7 ft tall. I can't seem to verify this giant of a man, but it's safe to say that big men tend to run in my family. And it's funny from my perspective because many people often think of Latinos as small in stature. They see me and it makes them do a double take. And, compared to many of the Latinos who play in the NFL, I'm on the smallish side. But the bottom line is that Latinos come in all shades and sizes, if you want to know the truth.

FLA: While we're on the Big-and-Tall subject let's talk about some of the bigger Latino players in the NFL—another set that do the lion's share of the work, but that ironically given their size don't seem to get that much attention. With the exception possibly of the well-known offensive tackle Anthony Muñoz (1958–) who brought his herculean 6 ft 6 inches and 280 pounds to the Cincinnati Bengals for 12 seasons (1980–1992), I'm thinking of players like the 6 ft 5 in, 247 pound Tony González who played for the Kansas City Chiefs (1997–2008) and the Atlanta Falcons (2009–present) as well as the 6 ft 3 inch, 225 pound linebacker Donnie Edwards (1973) who had a 14 season run with the Kansas City Chiefs (1996–2001; 2007–2009) and the Chargers (2002–2006). Guard for the Chargers (1987), the Broncos (1996–1998), among others, David Díaz-Infante (1964–) measured in at 6 feet 3 inches and nearly 300 pounds.

DOI: 10.1057/9781137403094

And, offensive tackle for the Panthers (1996–1999) and Cardinals (2000), Norberto Garrido (1972–) is a colossal 6 ft 6 inches and weighs in more than Muñoz at 336 pounds.

CG: They are all huge guys, and it should do away with any notion that all Latinos don't have the physical attributes to play in the NFL. Of course there are small-framed Latinos, just as there are small-framed African Americans, Whites, and Asians. That many people are surprised to see large framed Latinos shows just how powerful and pervasive the diminutive stereotypes of Latinos made famous by television and film truly are.

FLA: Maybe it's that brisket and corn you all eat in Texas, but several big Tejanos have played important offensive and defensive line positions. I'm thinking of 6 ft 4 inch, 308 pound Tejano, Jorge Diaz (1973–) who played offensive tackle for the Buccaneers (1996–1998) and Cowboys (1999). And, there's Roberto Garza (1979–) who played for the Atlanta Falcons (2001–2004) and the Bears (2005–present).

CG: There are few things so enjoyed in Texas as a well-smoked brisket! In all seriousness, though I've never formally met Roberto Garza, our paths did cross one at a collegiate track meet in Beaumont, Texas at Lamar University. In 1998 I was finishing my last year of eligibility at Sam Houston State University in Huntsville, Texas, and Garza was attending Texas A&M-Kingsville, where he played football as well as competed in the shot put and discus. When we competed against each other in the discus that day in Beaumont, I remember thinking just how big the guy was. I managed to win the competition that day, and I was ecstatic to learn later that Garza had become such a successful player in the NFL. So, yes, these are huge guys we're talking about, and that's coming from a larger-than-average guy.

FLA: As the story goes, a Marine recruiter tried to dash Garza's hopes of playing pro football, telling him "Mexican's don't play in the NFL"...

CG: I'm so glad Garza didn't listen to that guy! It's the sort of narrow-minded thinking Latinos deal with all the time. And it's not just with athletics. Anytime a Latino or Latina tries to break into a new area, he or she is confronted with the same sort of claptrap. The unfortunate thing is that, for all that Marine recruiter knew, Mexicans *didn't* play in the NFL. Just look at how we've had to work to uncover the invisibility of Latino players in the NFL. It's not that the recruiter was right, but he was probably basing his observation on his direct experience with the NFL.

DOI: 10.1057/9781137403094

But he must have been an inattentive fan if he didn't know of Anthony Muñoz, the Pro Football Hall of Famer who is, according to many, the greatest offensive lineman to play in the NFL. Garza is also an offensive lineman. If anything, the recruiter should've known better, but he was most likely relying on the kind of stereotypes we've been exposing in this book.

FLA: Colossal in size doesn't mean superhero invincibility. A lot of these guys suffer heavy physical damage on the field, including brain injury.

CG: It's a matter of physics. These larger bodies have the potential to generate greater forces and thus greater traumas.

FLA: We've begun to give shape to the diverse range of Latinos that have been transforming the corpus of game. There's also a regional range that comes into play. We talked about the urbanization of Latinos earlier in our *conversación*.

CG: Indeed there is a regional aspect in all of this. Many of the players we've discussed have originated from the American Southwest—particularly California. But we've also seen other major metro areas contribute Latino players to professional football.

FLA: The inclination in football appears to be following the national trend of Latinos—many of the Latinos playing in pro football hail from cities like San Jose, Los Angeles, Dallas, Houston, Tulsa, Tampa…In addition to San Jose denizens like Plunkett and Flores there are others like San Francisco born and Ontario (California) raised Anthony Muñoz, San Diego born and Ontario (California) raised Juan Roque (1974–) who played offensive tackle for the Detroit Lions (1997–1999) then played for the Toronto Argonauts (2001–2002). Tony González (1976–) was born and raised (single Latina mom) in Torrance, California. There's Tulsa born Tony Casillas (1963) who was defensive tackle for the Falcons (1986–1990) and who helped take the Cowboys to victory at the Super Bowl (1991–1993, 1997). And, there is the San Diego born and Burlington (Wisconsin) raised Antonio Ramiro "Tony" Romo (1980–) who quarterbacks for the Dallas Cowboys (2003–present).…

CG: It makes sense that we see Latino football players from cities where we find greater concentrations of Latinos in the population. A Latino football player out of Anchorage, Alaska or Fargo, North Dakota would be a rare thing because the numbers of Latinos in those areas are relatively

DOI: 10.1057/9781137403094

small. We would expect more Latino football players competing at elite levels in places like Houston, San Diego, Los Angeles, Chicago, New York, and Miami, for instance.

FLA: There are several Latino footballers that have come out of Boston and New York, too. I'm thinking of the Brooklyn born Nuyorican Marco Rivera (1972) who played 11 seasons as a guard in the NFL, first for the Green Bay Packers (1996–2004) then the Dallas Cowboys (2005–2006). And there's Stalin Colinet (1974–) who was the first Dominican American Latino to play in the NFL, from New York City, attended Boston College, then played defensive end for the Vikings (1997–1999, 2001), Browns (1999–2000), Jacksonville Jaguars (2002–2002).

CG: And then there's Victor Cruz (1986) who has become a star wide receiver for the New York Giants (2010–present). Cruz celebrates his Puerto Rican heritage, while simultaneously honoring his grandmother, by performing a salsa dance after he scores a touchdown. He was born in Paterson, New Jersey and attended the University of Massachusetts. It's a reminder that Latino NFL players are not just a part of the Southwest.

FLA: Along with Cruz, there are players like Rivera and Colinet as well as referees like Riveron—all of whom remind us, as you just pointed out, of the diverse range of cultural and historical backgrounds (Dominican, Puerto Rican, Cuban) that make up the umbrella group we've been calling Latino.

CG: Mexican-Americans, or Chicanos, comprise the largest aspect of the group we call Latinos (around 70%). But this has not stopped other Latino groups, such as the ones you just noted, from being a significant part of the NFL culture specifically, and American culture generally.

FLA: This isn't to say that football in the more rural areas is altogether out. Several important Latino players have come from the more rural regions of the U.S. There's the Nogales (Arizona) born Danny Villa (1964–) who played 12 seasons for the NFL, including as guard for the New England Patriots (1987–1991, 1997); and, there's Rock Springs (Wyoming) born Adam Archuleta (1977–) who was a defensive back for the St. Louis Rams (2001–2005), the Redskins (2006), and the Chicago Bears (2007).

CG: Whether we're talking about the impact of the NFL on urban or rural populations, let's remember that it is the most watched professional sport in the U.S. Football is also the most prominent sport played in high schools all across the country. In fact, rural communities who may not have much in

DOI: 10.1057/9781137403094

the way of entertainment venues have huge high school football fan bases. Recall the *Friday Night Lights* mindset of these rural and regional areas. Football is king of sports in America. And today things have progressed such that no matter where Latinos might be, they may finally have access to the pipeline we've been speaking about throughout our conversation.

FLA: Given that we're still seeing a relative few, can we even talk about regional and ethnic (within the Latino umbrella) trends here?

CG: I think it's still a little soon for that. Latinos comprise a very small percentage of NFL players and coaches in a given season, and that's an important point to consider. We've been stringing together an invisible tradition of Latinos in the NFL, and we've made the argument that it's significant. But if we look any single season of the NFL rather than the sum total of its history, we're still only talking about a relative handful of Latinos in the NFL: 1–2 per team at most. In the 2007 season there were 24 Latinos in the NFL, for instance; there are 32 teams currently.

FLA: Christopher, let's talk Latinos in football and *globalization*. As we already discussed, many Latino players in the early days had to cross the border into Canada to prove their value to the NFL. That is, on an individual level they crossed a border to make visible their athletic capital. Might we consider something like how the transnational Latino becomes a commodity in the athletic marketplace?

CG: Interestingly, I think the NFL is now trying to market its connection to Latino culture by selling its product (the game) to Latinos in the U.S. Isn't it amazing that the top-dog in American sports is trying to rebrand itself as a game with links to Latinidad? I mean, is it too cynical to say that the NFL didn't really want Latinos in the game for much of its history, but now that Latinos are comprising a growing percentage of the spending power in this country, the NFL suddenly wants to celebrate "Fútbol Americano" every September during Hispanic Heritage Month? Before it goes about selling Latino culture in Latin America, the NFL will continue to make the most of this untapped market in the U.S. That's not to say, however, that the NFL will not take its game across borders; it already has with regular-season games played in the U.K. and Canada, and exhibition games in Mexico. We should expect to see the NFL continue its outreach to other parts of the globe as well as within the U.S.

FLA: The CFL still seems to play an important role for Latinos. The undrafted quarterback from Gilroy (California) Jeff Garcia crossed over

DOI: 10.1057/9781137403094

into Canada to play for the Calgary Stampeders (1994–1998), crossing back over the border to take up with the 49ers (1999–2003), the Browns (2004), Lions (2005), Eagles (2006), then finally as starting quarterback for the Buccaneers (2007–2008)...

CG: O, Canada! I mean, it's a bit depressing to hear that Canada can lay a greater claim to Latinos in professional football than the NFL can. It's a bit infuriating, yet it makes me respect the Canadian brand of professional football all the more. Also, I'm glad you brought up Jeff Garcia—a light skinned, red haired Latino who was constantly badgered about, you guessed it, his height throughout his career, and later, his sexuality. But he had some terrific success in the NFL *after* four seasons in Canada. I guess if you're a Latino who aspires to play in the NFL, thank goodness for Canada!

FLA: As we saw when discussing the Latino kickers playing in the NFL, there have been many players who have crossed the border from South to North America.

CG: It does speak to the global nature of sports in general. Whether it's American football, basketball, the Olympics, and so on, athletes are globetrotting in pursuit of their athletic dreams. Just as many Latinos in the U.S. traveled north to play in Canada, Latin-Americans have managed to pursue football in the U.S. as well.

FLA: Athletes are put in the same category as professors and other skilled workers for H1B Visas...

CG: In effect, they get this special privilege because they have a valuable talent—valuable being the operative word. Think of how a professional athlete can contribute to the economy of the U.S. if they are given an H1B Visa. Our moral compass tells us this isn't right—that individuals wishing to come to America to work might get a *temporary* H2B Visa that allows them to work the backbreaking seasonal work in agribusiness, but a fashion model or professional athlete gets a kind of special treatment, just doesn't seem fair.

FLA: We as Latinos are living, breathing embodiments of border crossing. I think of David Díaz-Infante whose father was a Zapatista (Mexico) and whose mother was Finnish American...

CG: Díaz-Infante is the archetypical American immigrant story. His family was forced to come to America, and while he was here, Díaz-Infante channeled his stress and anxiety into the game of football. It helped that he was another one of these large Latinos you mentioned earlier—he played guard. And he was in the American Southwest where he found the right programs

DOI: 10.1057/9781137403094

and the right mentors that allowed him to develop his talent. Without those opportunities, Díaz-Infante would never have played in the NFL.

FLA: The founding of the World League of American Football is certainly a move to take football *global*. Latinos have played an important part in this, too. I think of Plunkett's draft into the World League of American Football in 1974. There were others like Mayen "Manny" Fernández, Efrén Herrera, David Díaz-Infante, Marco Rivera, and Norberto Garrido who either used the WLAF as a stepping stone into the NFL or who chose to step out of the NFL to have careers in the WLAF. For instance, Rivera found his niche with the Scottish Clamores; and Díaz-Infante used the Frankfurt Galaxy (1991–1992) as a stepping stone to find his feet once again (he had been injured while playing for the Broncos) back into the NFL to play for the Denver Broncos (1996–1998) then the Philadelphia Eagles (1999–2001) then back to the Broncos (2001).

CG: The push to globalize American football has been slow and steady, and it has yet to catch on—unlike, say, professional basketball. Some of that has to do with a world that has an appetite for the game of soccer—whose concept of time and scoring are completely at odds with American football. Also, consider the specialized gear one needs to play football. The gear is cost prohibitive for the youth of many nations of the world. And if the youth can't play it and develop a passion for it, the game will never be a significant part of a nation's sports identity.

FLA: We know for sure that American styled football has been in Mexico since the 1920s, and perhaps before. Mexico's college teams have been growing at a steady clip. (Today they number over 50). And in the late 1990s, football had become so popular in Mexico that more NFL games were broadcast there per week than in New York. In 2005, Mexico began regularly hosting NFL pre-season exhibition games.

CG: The Dallas Cowboys in particular has a strong connection to Mexico. Dallas often plays exhibition games there, and the team is wildly popular—among the most popular teams in all of Mexico. In general, the NFL is growing in popularity in America's neighbor to the south. And yet again I reference the NFL's current marketing of its sport to Latino audiences both at home and abroad.

FLA: What are we to make finally of the presence of Latinos in the NFL and the game's increased presence in the Americas? I wonder if Latinos in pro football continue to expand and thicken.

DOI: 10.1057/9781137403094

CG: I don't see how the Latino presence in the NFL will dissipate anytime soon. More and more Latinos are entering high profile collegiate football programs (think of quarterback Taylor Martinez at the University of Nebraska), and the current successes of Latinos in the NFL will motivate more Latino youth to pursue a career playing professional football. It will be interesting to observe and track Latinos in the NFL over the next ten years, say, until the year 2025. My guess is that Latinos will make up a larger percentage of the players, the coaches, and viewers than there are at the moment.

FLA: I wonder, too, if American football will grow deeper roots south of the Tortilla curtain—a climate that possibly makes the lighter gear of *fútbol* more suitable...

CG: As I noted a moment ago, I think the gear of American football makes the game cost prohibitive for the youth of certain nations. Unlike *fútbol*, where you really only need something that functions as a soccer ball, American football requires all sorts of equipment that is absolutely necessary for safety's sake. But I imagine kids in Mexico can play football the way I did as a kid—with a football and a few friends on an open patch of land. You can still develop a passion for playing the game without Under Armor- or Nike-brand gear.

FLA: Might we see a day, Christopher, when the pro football field looks more like soccer fields north and south of the Tortilla curtain—with more shades of brown. As new generations of Latinos come up through the ranks and with demographic weight bringing a certain economic pressure to the game (especially upper management?), it will be interesting to see what kind of transformations take place in and around the field.

CG: Many very important precedents have already been set. Latinos can play quarterback in the NFL. They can be offensive linemen. They can be receivers. They can be head coaches. They can play in the Super Bowl. They can coach a winning team in the Super Bowl. They can quarterback a team to victory in the Super Bowl. They can win the Super Bowl MVP. They can become the quarterback for the most valuable sports franchise in the world like Tony Romo of the Dallas Cowboys. They can become deserving Hall of Famers like Anthony Muñoz. They can become one of the greatest tight ends in history like Tony González. All of these things *needed* to happen in order for people—Latino or otherwise—to see that Latinos have a claim to this most American of games.

DOI: 10.1057/9781137403094

4

The Blitz...Heroes, Saviors, Saints, and Sinners

Abstract: *"The Blitz...Heroes, Saviors, Saints, and Sinners,"* considers the role of the community, the media, and capitalism generally in the rise and fall of Latino superstar players.

Frederick Luis Aldama and Christopher González. *Latinos in the End Zone: Conversations on the Brown Color Line in the NFL.* New York: Palgrave Macmillan, 2014.
DOI: 10.1057/9781137403094.

Frederick Luis Aldama: As we've discussed, questions of perception (misperception!) and representation have played an important role in the story of Latinos in the NFL. I'd like us to think specifically about how *actual* representations in the media have shifted in time. We could choose many examples, but there's certainly a difference between the representations of Latinos and racial Others like Cherokee Sonny Sixkiller in the 1970s to those in the 21st century...

Christopher González: Times have changed in terms of how football and celebrity culture have come together over the last few decades. In the 1970s there was still a kind of workman, blue-collar ethos to professional football despite the advent of the *fashonista* Joe Namath; few NFL quarterbacks have worn mink so well as "Broadway Joe," while on the sideline no less! In fact, Namath seems to be the start of NFL players, and particularly NFL quarterbacks, as celebrities rivaling the top movie stars of their day.

But not all NFL quarterbacks get the star treatment. Only the starting quarterbacks get top billing, and specifically those QBs of large profile teams—teams such as the New York Jets, the Dallas Cowboys, and the San Francisco 49ers. You don't often see the quarterback of the Tampa Bay Buccaneers on the cover of *GQ*, especially the early Buccaneers. As for Latino quarterbacks, they were typically featured on the cover of sports magazines as these dynamic, stoic individuals. Again I recall the *Sports Illustrated* cover with "The Toughest Chicano" Joe Kapp, gazing in the distance in mid snarl. How could he *not* be the toughest Chicano with a grimace like that?

FLA: It seems ironic that while there were certainly fewer Latinos in pro football in the 1970s, the early media representations of Latino and racially Othered football players were anchored firmly in the game. Both Sixkiller and Plunkett are in full regalia, and in action: Plunkett's wound up and about to throw the ball and Sixkiller's looks as if he just unstrapped after playing a serious game. Conversely, in Sanchez's pose for *GQ* we see him holding a ball, but seemingly as accouterment for his metrosexual look....

CG: Correct. Plunkett looks like he's about to complete a 60 yard pass. The picture of Sixkiller might have been taken just as he was about to take the field or head to the sideline. Such early images worked to reaffirm that these Latinos *belonged* in the game. It was the visual proof that Latinos were actually playing the game, not just holding a clipboard

DOI: 10.1057/9781137403094

on the sideline. By the time Sanchez entered the game, there was less a need to see a Latino in his uniform or on the field—recall that Flores and Plunkett had been there, done that. Also, it's notable that Sanchez is on the cover of *GQ* and not a sports magazine. He's not on the cover to sell to sports fans. It's another commodification of a Latino body, and another way for the NFL and Mark Sanchez to generate higher revenues. In truth, Sanchez has the kind of look that might make the cover of *GQ* even if he didn't happen to be the franchise quarterback for the New York Jets.

FLA: As we've discussed, the 1970s was a watershed moment for Latinos in pro football. It was a moment when we began to see Latinos on the cover of magazines, on MVP posters, and all variety of other media. In many ways, it was a time when Latinos could be *out* as Latino, but of course *out* within prescriptions of ethnicity. Today, Latinos seem increasingly matter of fact about their Latinidad. I'm thinking of Sanchez after his USC days and Tony Romo among many others.

CG: I've heard much more regarding Sanchez and his Latinidad than Romo, and I wonder if this has to do with their phenotypes and America's expectations of Latinos. I think, by and large, people expect Latinos to be of the brown variety—though we are all shades of skin color so that we can "look" White, Black, or Asian. Visually, Romo could "pass" for White more so than Sanchez. Thus, I think it's easy for fans and viewers to "forget" that Romo is Latino. I only remember seeing one overt mention of Romo's Latinidad explored since he's been the Cowboys' quarterback, and it was a piece done by ESPN. Except for that one instance, Romo's ethnicity is generally not raised in national outlets. That's not to say local media or smaller market publications don't explore this avenue of Romo's heritage. I'm speaking of the national image that has been crafted for both of these high-profile quarterbacks. Sanchez engages with issues of his Latinidad far more than Romo.

FLA: Perhaps we have come around, finally. In the past it was certainly the case monolingual Spanish or an accented English were used as markers of difference (discrimination, actually) along with phenotype (darker versus lighter skin).

CG: It's true that the darker Sanchez can be *loud and proud* about his Latinidad in ways that would not have been possible in earlier epochs. But we have to keep in mind too that he's more *GQ* model in bone structure than everyday *mestizo*...

DOI: 10.1057/9781137403094

FLA: Of course, being more free to be loud and proud concerning one's Latino heritage doesn't include *coming out* about all aspects of one's identity. I think of Terrell Owens' nuanced implication that Jeff Garcia was gay in *Playboy* magazine (September 2004). After this outing Garcia married *Playboy* playmate of 2004, Carmella DeCesare.

CG: The NBA just had a revelatory moment when Jason Collins announced his homosexuality. The NFL, as the banner-carrying manliest of sports, hasn't had a similar moment. There is a tremendous amount of homophobia in the NFL, its culture, and its fandom. Watch a sampling of commercials during the broadcast of an NFL game and it becomes clear the kind of *übermensch* the NFL money machine has in mind. An effeminate or homosexual man is anathema to the ethos of football. One of the most common insults I see on social media concerns Tony Romo and the fact that his surname rhymes with "homo." So, he is constantly belittled and emasculated by fans that don't like him. They cannot see that declaring him a homosexual because his name rhymes with a gay slur is asinine. More disturbingly, it signals how a man's homosexuality should preclude his ability to play in the NFL or disqualify him altogether in the minds of many fans.

This issue is reminiscent of what Terrell Owens did to Jeff Garcia's reputation, as you mention. Not only was Garcia's sexuality or lifestyle none of his business, but the matter of a man's sexuality should have nothing to do with how well he is able to play the game of football. To this day the rumors of Garcia's sexuality follow him, and I'm certain the fallout of this unfortunate incident will keep closeted homosexuals in the NFL quiet until long after their playing days are over. Although, in April of 2013, former Baltimore Ravens player Brendon Ayenbedajo , an outspoken supporter of marriage equality and gay rights, predicted that a handful of players might come out in the near future.

FLA: We've seen players come out as gay, but usually *after* their pro football careers have ended. I think of David Kopay and Esera "Mr. Aloha" Tuaolo. Recently, news has been made when straight players like Brett Favre and Tom Brady have publically supported gay rights generally, along with Ayenbedajo. Yet, the don't-ask-don't-tell modus operandi still seems fully in play.

CG: No one wants to be the first active player to announce his homosexuality. I imagine the fallout will be a media circus, and it is more than possible that such a player would lose potential earnings from sponsorships.

DOI: 10.1057/9781137403094

Those same advertisers who promote the *übermensch* football player and the fans who follow these players are keen to avoid anything that hinders that ethos. It will be a courageous, life-altering move for the player who makes the decision to come out while playing in the NFL, but it will be the right move in the eyes of history.

We should add an addendum to our exploration of sexuality in the NFL. Remember what happened to Manti Te'o in his final year with the Notre Dame Fighting Irish. He was riding the wave of an amazing season, a Heisman Trophy finalist who played for a national championship against Alabama. But weeks before the championship game, it came to light that his girlfriend, whom Te'o claimed had died earlier in the season, did not exist. Suddenly the world learned that Te'o's relationship had been entirely online with a girl who was a conjuration. In the public's thirst for a rational explanation, some conjectured that Te'o was gay. There he was on Katie Couric's show, awkwardly denying that he was gay. In truth, if he were gay, what did that have to do with his ability to play at a high level? The controversy may have cost Te'o hundreds of thousands if not millions in earnings after he ended up being drafted at a much lower spot than many would have predicted just a few months earlier. It's a reminder that the NFL is a business, and in it, image is everything.

FLA: Speaking of image, while playing for USC Sanchez embraced his *Latinidad*—his Mexicanness announced in various ways including mouth guard with a Mexican flag—and became a hero to Latinos. To others, he was told: "Go back to Mexico"...

CG: In professional sports, loyalty knows no bounds. Neither does the hate. There are some teams that some NFL fans just hate. People will look for any reason to demoralize or denigrate a hated team. The days of Mark Sanchez at USC were good ones, and Trojans fans were riding high as a top-tier program. Using his Mexican heritage against him, sadly, does not surprise me. Remember a few chapters ago I talked about the vitriol and hate directed at an 11-year-old mariachi singer who did nothing more than sing the "Star-Spangled Banner." In our conversation we've outlined the struggles Latino players have faced, and in sum it sounds like those troubles are a thing of the past. However, social media has brought out closeted racism like never before. It used to be the old saying went, "Everyone's got an opinion." Today, seemingly it's, "Everyone's got a racist opinion." Thank goodness for the various websites that publicly shame these people for all to see.

DOI: 10.1057/9781137403094

FLA: With Latinos left out of the history books traditionally, the Latino community has *made* its heroes. From Pancho Villa to Joaquin Murieta to Gregorio Cortéz to Jim Plunkett to Anthony Muñoz (his hometown Ontario even named a park after him) to Juan Roque to Mark Sanchez...

CG: The Latino community is often *forced* to make its own heroes because so few Latinos become heroes to the hegemony. Gregorio Cortéz became the ultimate hero because he was just an average guy minding his business and was forced to take action against the white hegemony. Pancho Villa was the revolutionary who made even powerful men quake in their boots. There's something of the underdog in the Latino ethos, and we appreciate an underdog story more than most. But someone once said that the gods did not fashion us in their image but rather we fashioned the gods after our own. In other words, we like to see something of ourselves in those we worship on Sundays—be that in the church or the football stadium.

FLA: We've mentioned already the lack of Latinos honored in that space (church?) of the proverbial gods in Canton, Ohio known as the Pro Football Hall of Fame. We know well until there is a diversification of the nominating committee, deserving Latinos will be left out. This doesn't mean that Latinos have passively sat by. In Ontario they named that park: "Anthony Muñoz Hall of Fame Park."

CG: Anthony Muñoz is an interesting case. He is one of the true greats of the game, and arguably one of the greatest to play the position of tackle. He was an 11-time Pro Bowler and played in two Super Bowls; his Cincinnati Bengals lost twice to the 49ers. It seems natural that the community of Ontario would name a park after him—and that Muñoz is one of these proverbial gods in the Hall of Fame. He should be. But Plunkett was selected to nine Pro Bowls, quarterbacked the winning team in the Super Bowl (twice!), and has a nearly 70% passer rating for his career. Plunkett should be in the Hall of Fame without a doubt. For some reason, the 40+ people who comprise the Selection Committee think the Pro Football Hall of Fame is better without Plunkett. I get riled when I think of it because it seems like such an injustice. Tom Flores has doubled John Madden's Super Bowl coaching victories, and yet he, too, remains outside Canton. You mentioned that Latinos have to make their own heroes. It seems we have to because we can't rely on others to do it for us.

DOI: 10.1057/9781137403094

FLA: Those like Muñoz who've become heroes to the Latino community give back. Muñoz established a foundation in 2002 to encourage business development in areas that promote youth health. Many others have become active members of health foundations: Tony González with the Kidney Foundation and an organization that works with hospitalized children (Shadow Buddhism). Tony Romo with United Way, Make-A-Wish Foundation, and the SPCA. Roberto Garza also with United Way as well as various homeless and Big Brother and Big Sister youth programs. Danny Villanueva established a football scholarship at his alma mater New Mexico State University.

CG: While a lot of professional players give back to the community, Latinos, as a historically marginalized group, understand how important those early resources are for kids. It's a terrific thing to see, and it also serves to inspire children. But we need to see more mentoring and engagement by Latinos in the community, not just from professional football players but also by professionals in all areas.

FLA: Absolutely, Christopher. I wonder if the making of role models isn't too easily supplanted by our love of heroes—not just as Latinos, but Americans generally. I love it that we have a Plunkett, a Muñoz—even a Sanchez. We love our heroes—heroes *as* saviors perhaps even more.

CG: I don't know if it's the idea of a savior so much as the idea of representation. Someone like Plunkett or Sanchez or Romo speaks to a Latino's sense of stake in the game. It gives us a sense of belonging and ownership of professional football, despite those haters who shout, "Go back to Mexico" from the rafters. Historically, Latinos have constantly been told they don't belong, despite the thousands upon thousands of Latinos who can trace their ancestry in this land far before there was a United States of America, so that's nothing new. It has happened and will continue to happen the more we break ground in areas people never expected to see us. Also, it's the need to want to see something of ourselves in the heroes we create. A little Latino boy growing up in west Texas may have a hard time believing he can be John Elway, but he might believe he can be Jim Plunkett. Those sorts of thing really do matter.

FLA: Umberto Eco considers how the ultimate hero, the comic book character Superman, is an immutable archetype. Yet, as he overcomes obstacles that threaten humankind, we expect him to experience a growth of character. Superman's characterization is as a fixed-mythological figure yet our interest as readers is in his transformation—his kinesis of

DOI: 10.1057/9781137403094

consciousness, if you will. This presents irreconcilable tensions between the characterization of Superman and our expectation of the character's psychology. I wonder if in our making of Latino heroes out of Plunketts and Sanchezes might present a similar set of tensions.

CG: I'm glad that you mentioned Superman. For such a popular character, it has been hard for Hollywood to make an exceptional Superman film. I'm thinking of the most recent reboot with Zack Snyder's *Man of Steel* starring Henry Cavill, and the mixed reception it received. Many called it boring or too action filled. But what makes bringing Superman to film so difficult is that he is essentially a god, and we're not interested in invincibility. We want even the best of us to face adversity and *overcome* that adversity. For Superman the challenge has always been his coming to terms with his dual nature (Krypton/Earth) and the existential search for who he is. How can Superman experience conflict enough to be changed by it?

You mention Plunkett and Sanchez. I would bring up Sanchez and Romo. These two quarterbacks receive most of the "overrated" criticisms among active quarterbacks. Being completely objective, we have to conclude that the two players are extraordinarily gifted. Romo has one of the fastest releases of the ball the game has ever seen, and it is seen as a correlation of quarterbacking talent. By contrast, see conversations of Tim Tebow's disastrously slow release of the ball due to his poor mechanics and long wind up. Sanchez also has top-tier physical skills. And yet I find it interesting that the two most maligned quarterbacks in the NFL right now happen to be Latino. I'm not suggesting the two issues are related, but it is nonetheless the case. At this point the only thing that can save their reputations as quarterbacks is a series of Super Bowl wins. Today's quarterbacks are measured by how many Super Bowl rings they have. Until Romo and Sanchez win games at the highest level, they're going to experience all the conflict they ever imagined. Just like Superman.

FLA: For someone like the Scottish essayist Thomas Carlyle, the figure of the hero is free, outward, and courageous. However, Carlyle might be thinking too parochially—too white. Those heroes identified in Latino history seem to be the rebels like *la malinche*, Hidalgo and the Bros Aldama, Gregorio Cortéz, among many others. That is, they are rebels and revolutionaries. Perhaps this is how we should be thinking about Latino heroes in the NFL.

DOI: 10.1057/9781137403094

CG: It would be easier to think of Latino players in the NFL as rebels and revolutionaries if they acted more like it. We have two extremes here, and I know we'll get to both in more depth momentarily. On the one hand you have someone like Romo, an undrafted player out of a small university football program. By most standards, he shouldn't even be in the NFL, much less the face of the *world's* most valuable sports franchise (according to *Forbes*). His rise began out of the blue as he replaced former number one pick Drew Bledsoe at halftime against the Washington Redskins. Coach Bill Parcells made the move because he had no choice. But suddenly Romo thrived, and he became an overnight sensation. Before long he was in commercials for ESPN and dating Jessica Simpson. Though he played less than a full season, that first year Romo garnered a Pro Bowl selection. But it has taken many years for Romo to emerge as the player who is in control of the Dallas Cowboys. He seems to acquiesce and won't take matters into his own hands like Brett Favre or Tom Brady. It's as if he is simply happy to be there at times. There is little of the rebel or revolutionary in him thus far.

On the other hand, you have someone who has taken the rebel image to the extreme: Aaron Hernandez currently alleged to have committed murder. Hernandez is a player who personified a rebellious persona and seemed to have actually lived his life in the same way. Clearly, if Hernandez is found guilty of murder, that's not the kind of hero anyone would want to follow.

FLA: Might there be a savior-impulse to this entire hero making with Latinos? I think of how some of our heroes have fallen, but the winds of something that we might identify as *belief* seem to hold them up. Remember when Tony Romo fumbled that snap and instead of getting it to the goal line was tackled, ending the season for the Cowboys. Yet Romo just signed a six-year extension with the Cowboys (to a tune of $108 million). And the 2012 season proved a comedy of errors for Sanchez now known for his invention of the "butt fumble"; while he's to play second fiddle to Geno Smith, the Jets let the general manager and offensive coordinator go but signed Sanchez—and to a tune of $8.25 million whether he gets off the bench or not. Do we need to believe at all cost that there is a Superman who overcome and who will save us?

CG: It was only a matter of time before we got to all of these fumbles in our *conversación*. I'll reiterate my claim that Sanchez and Romo are exceptionally talented. That said, they have made some of the most

DOI: 10.1057/9781137403094

infamous plays in NFL history at the absolute worst possible moments. The result is that these two players are seen as not being "clutch" or that they will never win the big game because they'll manage to lose the game somehow. Romo has many more successes in the fourth quarter than failures, but the image has been crafted that he will do something to blow the game. When Romo fumbled that snap against the Seattle Seahawks in the playoffs, he set in motion all of this talk that he couldn't win in the playoffs. If Romo never wins a Super Bowl, that botched snap will live in the archive of NFL Films, ready to be shown whenever his name is mentioned.

Sanchez of late has me wondering what has happened to him. He came to the NFL on fire, and quickly led the Jets to two consecutive AFC Championship games. But since then he's been in a death spiral. The so-called butt fumble, like Romo's botched snap, is destined to outlast Sanchez's playing career and beyond. But no one, except for NBC's Cris Collinsworth, bothered to notice just how instrumental New England's Vince Wilfork was in making the play happen. Wilfork manhandled Jets' guard Brandon Moore and launched him into the path Sanchez was taking. But Sanchez is the high-profile quarterback who will get all of the criticism for any of the team's mistake, just as Romo will take the blame for every wrong move the Dallas Cowboys make. However, Romo and Sanchez are both paid by teams who hope they will become the Superman the teams have hoped for.

FLA: I sometimes wonder how much it is a case of making and worshiping heroes or simply our love of the Horatio Alger protean narrative. We experience all sorts of emotional ups and downs when reading Tom Flores's *Fire and the Iceman*, Jorge Prieto's *The Quarterback Who Almost Wasn't*, and Plunkett's *The Jim Plunkett Story*. However, they are all ultimately up-from-the-bootstraps success stories. Take Plunkett's story. We feel the pangs of his down-and-out life as he recounts an early childhood filled with his taking on odd jobs (gas station attendant, grocery clerk, physical laborer) to help support his family; his mother was blind and father became progressively blind. Then we experience the uplift when we learn that he was recognized as having a special talent when at age 14 he could hurl a football over 60 yards. We feel the anger and frustration of his early days as a Latino at Stanford as well as a deep satisfaction when he recounts how he was taken off the bench to become a superhero quarterback for the Raiders when Dan Pastorini fractured his leg.

DOI: 10.1057/9781137403094

CG: It does seem to be the rags-to-riches story that people love so much. You mentioned Plunkett's story, which is inspirational whether you are Latino or not—but *especially* if you are Latino. And I think that's what initially propelled Romo to his meteoric rise as Dallas Cowboys quarterback. There are few positions in American sports that have such a white-hot spotlight on them—Yankees second baseman and Lakers guard might be comparable. Romo was this undrafted quarterback, one-time third stringer on the Cowboys roster who vaulted into the limelight on Monday Night Football. He was dynamic, a redux of Brett Favre but younger, and the media desperately wanted a star at the quarterback position in Dallas. It's good for business. And so early on Romo seemed like one of these Horatio Alger stories. But let's not dismiss just how much people love to tear down their idols. Once Romo botched that snap in Seattle, he became an easy target.

FLA: Our Latino heroes don't easily disappear once their pro football careers come to a close. Some even continue to be heard and seen from the sidelines on TV, film, and radio. Juan Roque, David Díaz-Infante, Flores, and Plunkett have all been (and some continue to be) radio commentators. Archuleta and his former wife *Playboy* playmate even appeared on the TV show *Football Wives* on *E!* Tony González appeared in TV shows like *Arliss* (2000) and *One Tree Hill* (2010). Fears appeared as a pilot in the Humphrey Bogart film, *Action in the North Atlantic.* Sáenz worked as a stunt man in several films and as double for Anthony Quinn. And, Kapp made cameos and played minor roles in football-themed films like *The Longest Yard, Semi-Tough,* among many others.

CG: Many Latinos have indeed been able to translate their football success into minor successes in other media outlets. Anthony Muñoz became a longtime football analyst and commentator, and that's the route most former players take once their playing career comes to a close.

FLA: The silver screen imagined Latinos playing football long before our presence. I'm thinking of Cuban-American musician and actor Desi Arnaz who plays Manuelito, the Latino college football player who literally falls over himself when he first sees the blue-eyed southern belle Connie (Lucille Ball) in *Too Many Girls* (1940).

CG: And yet the media and film history have immortalized the story not so much as being one of the first films to showcase a Latino character as a football player (and conga player), but as the first time that

DOI: 10.1057/9781137403094

Desi and Lucille met, married, then cooked up what has become a central ingredient in the mainstream's mythology of the hot-tempered Latino. Remember that *I Love Lucy* ran for nearly the whole decade of 1950s—with reruns continuously thereafter.

FLA: As you've already brought up, just as we have our Latino heroes, we also have those who fall from grace. Perhaps it's more accurate to say that we have our *saints* and *sinners*. No two players could exemplify this opposition more than Sanchez and Aaron Hernandez: Sanchez as Latino good-boy next door versus Hernandez as the dangerous gangbanger from the hood.

CG: A tale of two Latinos, indeed. Again, we have to keep in mind that the sports market is ratings driven. That's not necessarily a bad thing, but I think it's important to keep that in mind when we see how sports networks such as Fox Sports, NBC Sports, and ESPN cover Tony Romo, Mark Sanchez, and Aaron Hernandez. There is always an impulse by the media to turn what happens on and off the field into a certain kind of narrative that we are familiar with—such as the "kid next door" or "vato loco gangbanger" that helps generate interest. Unfortunately, that impulse oversimplifies these complex individuals.

FLA: The Latino community and the media at large gravitate toward this saint vs. sinner narrative. We see it in pro baseball (the saint turned sinner Alex Rodriguez) and also the NFL. The media transformed Norberto Garrido into a bad-boy news story in 1997 when it leaked that he'd punched a fellow player, quarterback Kerry Collins of the Panthers, in response to Collin's use of a racial slur. Recently, when news hit that murder charges were brought against tight end Aaron Hernandez of the New England Patriots, Geraldo Rivera remarked that the NFL had a *gang problem*.

CG: ¡Ay, Geraldo! That man says some of the most outrageous things and doesn't seem to learn from having said them. I think a more responsible answer than Rivera's is to say the NFL has a *control* issue. These players are treated like royalty, and before long they begin to think that the rules and laws don't apply to them. Having body art doesn't make a person a gangbanger. But when we have so many players who grew up in impoverished communities and suddenly become multimillionaires overnight, control over one's environment and life becomes crucial. The NFL understands this, and it now compels rookies to attend seminars that detail how to control themselves. I think this is an instance of the NFL protecting its

DOI: 10.1057/9781137403094

investment in these players, and it's also an issue of protecting the brand. They call it "protecting the shield," a reference to the NFL logo.

FLA: Along with the seeming need for *sinners* there's a seeming need to pathologize, especially those Latino Icarus figures that've reached too high. Before conviction or evidence, the news of Aaron Hernandez focused on the likely pathology that grew as a result of the early death of his father and his growing up with single mother.

CG: It's a push to make these players somehow deficient. Interestingly, it again aligns with the Horatio Alger narrative *and* the deviant narrative. ESPN makes hay of those players who overcame drugs, a broken home, the loss of a parent, and so on. It furthers the players' exceptional and superheroic qualities. But the same sorts of things are used to "explain" why an NFL player goes wrong. Both types of narratives are built on the tropes of the minority lifestyle as different from the norm, and either the player manages to overcome these seeming hardships or ultimately can never outrun them. It's a very specific kind of narrative manipulation.

FLA: We have seemingly become accustomed to sacrificial narratives— those prototype narratives identified by Patrick Hogan whereby there is the disobeying of a higher order (god in earlier iterations) that results in communal devastation; this can only be reversed through communal sacrifice. Might it be the case that those Latino pro footballers have been made into modern-day sacrificial victims as a promise to restore balance to the community...the nation.

CG: You referenced Icarus a moment ago, and I think it's a good myth to invoke. King Minos imprisoned Daedalus, along with his son Icarus. Daedalus fashioned their escape with artificial wings and warned his son not to go too high or too low. Icarus could not be kept from soaring as high as he wanted, and he plummeted to his death when the wax in his manufactured wings melted. Icarus paid a price for his transgression, and Daedalus paid also with the loss of his son. Perhaps people view with eagerness the fall of these NFL players as a sign that they had overachieved. That is not to say these players shouldn't be held personally responsible for misfortunes of their own creating. However, we must always interrogate how the media shapes these narratives for public consumption. It is not enough that Hernandez has allegedly made some egregious errors of judgment. The media must use folk psychology and punditry to explain his deviance, which ultimately incriminates the Latino community that produced Hernandez as well.

DOI: 10.1057/9781137403094

FLA: With the media's representation of Sanchez and Hernandez we see embodied the Latino male *as* body (and not mind) as at once dangerous and sexual.

CG: True, but let's not forget that Sanchez and Hernandez are very much complicit in this representation as well. Think of Victor Cruz of the New York Giants, an Afrolatino who has been an NFL darling for a few years now, especially after helping the Giants win the Super Bowl in 2012. He's been featured on the cover of *Latina* magazine, and he's also done somewhat campy commercials for Campbells' Chunky soup. He has so far made a conscious effort to avoid the "dangerous" and "sexual" image like that of Hernandez and Sanchez. Cruz has managed to embrace his Latino heritage—he speaks fluent Spanish—and yet has successfully avoided the sort of commodification you identify, Frederick.

It makes me wonder about the complicity of Latino NFL players in the sorts of narratives the media generate. It seems to me that NFL players wield a lot of clout, especially if they perform well on the field. As Latinos become a greater aspect of the NFL game, they should take a page from the Jim Plunketts and Victor Cruzes of the game.

FLA: Cruz seems to occupy a middle ground with Sanchez at one end of the Latino body spectrum (seductive) and Hernandez at the other (dangerous and discomforting).

CG: Definitely. It's also important to remember that these images are *staged*. That is to say, they are not pictures of these Latino players as they walk off the field or sit in a restaurant. When we see pictures of beautiful women clad in the tiniest of thongs every year in the *Sports Illustrated* "Swimsuit Edition," or *ESPN the Magazine*'s "The Body Issue" where athletes wear no clothing at all, we know we're seeing the models and athletes as idealized. The photos were not taken surreptitiously; the athletes participated in the photo shoots. So, while the photos of Sanchez and Hernandez are respectively seductive and discomforting, we have to keep in mind that they also participate in the promulgation of these sorts of images. In essence, Sanchez and Hernandez *own* the images they have helped create. Victor Cruz occupies a normal middle zone within the continuum (hypersexual to hyperdangerous) because he doesn't participate in the media's shaping of his image in the way Sanchez and Hernandez do.

FLA: Of course, the Latino players are not the only brown bodies sexualized by the media. Think of those Latinas in the Raiderettes and Dallas

DOI: 10.1057/9781137403094

Cowboys Cheerleaders—the latter included Demi Lovato's mom, Dianna De La Garza, known as Diana Hart (1982–1983).

CG: The Dallas Cowboys Cheerleaders in particular have long been sexualized bodies in the NFL. They are a perfect example of how the NFL caters to the *übermensch* ethos of its fan base. It has crafted an image of masculinity that engages in physical contact, alcohol consumption, nationalism, and idealized, sexualized women. The NFL sells peak human perfection, whether in the form of the NFL players we adore or the cheerleaders we long for.

FLA: Christopher, perhaps this returns us to that age-old question: are the Latina cheerleaders victims or careful strategists using their brown bodies to empower themselves within a patriarchal system.

CG: As I mentioned with the images of Sanchez and Hernandez, cheerleaders—Latina or otherwise—participate in how their bodies are used. One has only to watch a few episodes of *Dallas Cowboys Cheerleaders: Making the Team* to understand just how difficult it is to become an NFL cheerleader. The show also demonstrates just how aware the women are that their physical beauty is a product for consumption. That the cheerleaders are able to participate and, to a large extent, control how their body is commodified is an empowering move within a patriarchal system. It doesn't make the use or abuse of their bodies right, but it does give them the power to participate in the NFL if they so choose.

FLA: Keep in mind that the embrace of the brown (or other colored body) as cheerleader that we might take for granted today was certainly not the case during earlier times. What's interesting about Juanita Carpenter (her married name) was not so much that she was the first twirler (majorette) to lead a marching band in a gold sequined like swimsuit (Purdue University, 1954) but that she was Latina. She had blonde hair after having forgotten to wash the bleach out the night before.

CG: Latinas have had a struggle with the impulse to "whitewash" themselves in cinema and other public venues. Famously, Margarita Carmen Cansino had to lighten her hair and become Rita Hayworth during her film career. And consider the exemplar for American beauty and female sex today: Marilyn Monroe, who had to change her name and bleach her hair a platinum blonde. The disintegration of Monroe's self-esteem as a result of the pressures she felt concerning her weight undoubtedly led to her overdose in 1962.

DOI: 10.1057/9781137403094

Concerning NFL cheerleaders specifically, it's a thorny issue to say the least. NFL cheerleaders exist, and as far as they exist, it is empowering to see women from all demographics in the mix. As a father of two daughters, I dislike how women's bodies are commodified and sexualized. However, let's not fool ourselves into believing that all beautiful women are considered equally beautiful. Much of America still privileges the blond haired blue-eyed beauty as "All American." Recall the horrible comments hurled at Gabrielle Douglas, the first-ever African American winner of the all-around gold medal in Olympic gymnastics in 2012. Her looks, and particularly her hair, became the *cause célèbre* in the U.S. rather than her record-setting athletic achievements. Our conception of beauty has been and will remain one of the areas of contestation where issues of race are concerned.

FLA: Can we even talk about heroes when there are so many puppeteers. I'm thinking not just about the endorsers and owners of the NFL teams, but also the agents that are also making a profit off the players…

CG: My answer is a flat-out "No." All who participate in the NFL—players, coaches, cheerleaders, and so on, are all participants in a moneymaking business. There is much talk about heroism in the media, and the truth is that the real heroes rarely make it onto our televisions. The teams, the networks, the agents, they all make money from the athletes. The athletes in turn work the system to their advantage to make as much money as they can. And I can't fault anyone trying to make the most money they can legally make on their own talents and attributes within a system. The trap here is thinking that NFL players are either all powerful or helpless victims. They are neither.

FLA: Should we be considering the NFL as a modern-day iteration of Old Massie's plantation…

CG: Some would argue that, and many have done so. I'd be careful in supporting the idea that a capitalist enterprise where those who perform the labor are most often millionaires is akin to a slavery plantation where the labor was legally chattel. It does a disservice to those who suffered and died under slavery.

However, I would agree with the idea that the NFL is an engine of wealth that is designed to flourish and grow. It will always do what is good for business. If it were good for business to exclude minority players, then it would do so. If it is now good for business to include players of color, then it will do so. Further, I think the NFL has shown that it

DOI: 10.1057/9781137403094

cares about its players mostly from an investment and branding aspect and cares less about them after they can no longer contribute on the field. If it cared about the wellbeing of the players after their careers were over, the NFL would have taken greater steps to prevent such debilitating injuries. So, I wouldn't go so far as to compare it to a plantation, but I will say that the NFL treats the players and their talents as a commodity.

FLA: With their $5–25 million a year contracts NFL players make money that most mortals would never make many lifetimes over. However, given how much *is* made by the owners, advertisers, endorsement companies, can we still talk about exploited labor based on exchange and surplus value.

CG: I think we can talk about it in terms of what happens to the athletes *after* their careers are over. Remember, most of these players are retired in their mid-30s. Quite often, the mega wealth they earned in their playing years is depleted due to mismanagement or poor planning. Couple that with the physical ramifications of playing the game, and we start to understand the sort of obligation the NFL ought to have for their players *for the rest of their lives.* In that sense, we can talk about exploited labor. Consider how many former NFL players have declared bankruptcy, for instance. These players are drafted as very young men in their early 20s, and the NFL ought to take the responsibility to be more proactive for the wellbeing of the players. The NFL has gotten better in this respect, but many of these changes have come because the NFL Players Association has pushed for them.

FLA: At different moments in their careers, many Latino players have chosen to go the no-agent route. I think of Adam Archuleta, David Díaz-Infante, Jorge Diaz, Donnie Edwards, Antonio X. Gonzalez, Tony Romo...

CG: Perhaps this comes from necessity. For instance, Romo was not drafted in the 2003 NFL draft. He was essentially a free agent and did his best to negotiate his own contracts early on. For his $108 million extension, however, Romo did indeed allow his agent, R. J. Gonser, to handle the negotiations.

FLA: And, today we see that Latinos are not only on the field, but owners of companies—and teams. Tom Flores became president and general manager of the Seattle Seahawks in 1989. And, Marc Anthony and Jennifer Lopez along with Gloria and Emilio Estefan were part owners of the Miami Dolphins.

DOI: 10.1057/9781137403094

CG: It's a very important step for Latinos in the game. It is the ownership that steers the direction of the league. With more Latinos in positions of ownership and leadership in the NFL, the greater the Latino voice will be as the league continues to develop.

FLA: With Sanchez in *GQ* and Latinos and Romo (with Jessica Simpson) in *People* (July 13, 2009), among just a few examples, the kind of attention we received in bygone days seems rather innocent. How different it is for kids playing the video game, *Madden NFL 09 En Español* that featured the colossal Chicago Bears guard Roberto Garza on its cover to those trading cards of Fears (his came in a Wheaties box in 1951), Flores, and Plunkett.

CG: We might not be surprised to see prominent Latino NFL players on trading cards or cereal boxes, but to see them on the cover of *GQ* and *People* truly heightens our exposure. It sends the message that Latinos are very much a part of this huge enterprise of professional football. It also is a reminder that we are important shapers of American culture, and that we are not simply passive recipients shaped *by* that culture. We are working toward a day when Latinos on the covers of these sorts of magazines no longer seem like a rare exception.

FLA: Christopher, perhaps we should close by emphasizing the significant place of Latinos in the NFL—a sport that is very much fueled by capitalism. Perhaps the memorabilia manufactured that features Latinos best captures this. We have a greater Latino presence on the field and in the artifacts that represent this such as the MVP posters. While it is important that we see represented individuals like Plunkett prominently featured below, owners of the NFL teams today know well that Latino consumers have a $1.3 trillion buying potential.

CG: In short, that is really where we are at the moment. The surge of Latinos—in both population numbers and as a buying public—is without question a key reason why the NFL has begun to market itself to Latino audiences. Along with that, we have every reason to expect greater numbers of Latino players in the NFL. As a business, why wouldn't the NFL consider these factors in how it chooses to brand and market itself moving forward?

I think we've begun to uncover the invisible history of Latinos in the NFL over the course of our *conversación*, and I'm confident that the presence of Latinos will only become more and more palpable in the years to come.

DOI: 10.1057/9781137403094

5
Three Latino Legends: Snapshot by Interview

Abstract: *"Three Latino Legends: Snapshot by Interview,"
includes conversations we conducted with three Latino
football pioneers: Joe Kapp, Tom Flores, and Jim Plunkett. We
turn to our elders to learn from their wealth of experience and
wisdom as significant shapers in the history of the NFL.*

Frederick Luis Aldama and Christopher González. *Latinos
in the End Zone: Conversations on the Brown Color Line in
the NFL*. New York: Palgrave Macmillan, 2014.
DOI: 10.1057/9781137403094.

Joe Kapp

Frederick Luis Aldama & Christopher González: You have a very important story to tell, Joe.

Joe Kapp: Which one?

A&G: Your life as a Latino who grew up to play football for Cal, the CFL, the NFL, then as a great coach. The seed for all this was planted somewhere in your youth. You were born in Santa Fe, New Mexico, and as a child you moved with your family to California…

Kapp: Well, like many people, we came to California because there was no work in Santa Fe, New Mexico. The Southwest was a dust bowl, so people left to find work in California. When we arrived in California, we landed in San Fernando, one block off of what became Highway 99. We lived on Hollister Street—just down the road from the San Fernando Mission. It was the leadership of my mother, Florence Eufracia García Chávez, which brought the family to California. She has always been a great leader. She's up in Heaven organizing the angels to sing together at this moment.

A&G: The odds seemed to be stacked against you, living in other parts of California like Salinas.

Kapp: When we moved from San Fernando to Salinas, the California lettuce belt, we lived with other pickers, Okies, Arkies, blacks and whites and browns and purples. In the fifth grade a bigger kid called me "a dirty Mexican." Later I went back and found him and really whaled on him.

A&G: You helped raise your siblings, too.

Kapp: I was the eldest so I helped my mother. Her work was in the food business. She was a superior waitress in east Salinas where I spent much of my youth. I must say it was a great youth. The people that we associated with went on to have great lives. One of my best pals, if not my best pal, was Everett Alvarez, the first pilot shot down in Vietnam, and the longest held American prisoner of war. We played sports together. We were in the band together. He got the last trumpet and I had to settle for a tuba—or, sousaphone as they call it.

A&G: You ended up going to high school in Newhall, California.

Kapp: Yes, I achieved a certain amount of success at Hart High School in my studies and in sports such as football, basketball, and baseball. It was in high school that the door of opportunity opened. I should

DOI: 10.1057/9781137403094

also add that I owe much of my success in school to my mother whose great wisdom pointed me in the direction of speaking English. She knew how important it was to speak English in the world that we were living in.

A&G: Did you have any Latino athletes that served as role models when you were young?

Kapp: Even though we didn't play tennis in our neighborhood, we were aware of the world's number one tennis player, Pancho Gonzales. There was also the Puerto Rican golfer Chi Chi Rodríguez. But there was also Joe Louis. We thought of him as Joe *Luis*, the Heavyweight Champion of the World.

It really didn't matter what nationality you were or what your background was. We loved all sports. There was no TV then. Whatever sports we watched were at the movies on Saturday morning. This was when you could get in with a ten-cent ticket to watch the sports highlights and a good John Wayne movie.

A&G: You did well in your studies in high school and managed to get a basketball scholarship to go to UC Berkeley…

Kapp: I was a pretty good basketball player at Hart High School in Newhall. Our team was a very good basketball team and I made All CIF [California Interscholastic Federation] in basketball. But also split my time as a quarterback playing for the Hart High School Indians.

After having lived in places like Salinas for part of my life, I really appreciated my days at Cal with both football coach Lynn "Pappy" Waldorf [at Cal from 1947–1956] and then Pete Elliott [at Cal from 1957–1959] as well as probably the greatest basketball coach of all time, Pete Newell [at Cal from 1954–1960]. As it turns out, I lettered in basketball in 1956 and 1957 in which the Bears made two NCAA tournament appearances and led Cal to the Rose Bowl in 1959, losing to Iowa.

A&G: There certainly weren't many if any Latinos playing in college or pro football at the time.

Kapp: There weren't any Latinos playing football that I knew of when I was going to school. There was Sam "The Rifle" Etcheverry who was also from New Mexico. He went up to Canada and played for the Montreal Alouettes of the Canadian Football League. Whether or not there were other Latino players didn't matter. I was ready, and nothing was going to hold me back.

DOI: 10.1057/9781137403094

A&G: From Cal you ended up going to Canada to play football for the Calgary Stampeders. You mention Sam "The Rifle" Etcheverry, but there were other Latinos who would first go to the CFL before returning to the U.S. to play in the NFL. Were Latinos being discriminated against in the U.S. pro leagues?

Kapp: I do not believe this was about racial prejudice. However, there is a story here. There was a person that did not deal honestly with me that led to my trip to Canada; this same person also undermined my coming home to the U.S. (I wanted to go to San Diego or Houston.) I was a First Team All-America selection (1958), finished fifth in the 1958 Heisman Trophy voting, led California to a Rose Bowl, and was a member of the Cal Athletic Hall of Fame. Yet, I was 217th in the draft by the Washington Redskins. I never will say it was prejudice. But I will say that what happened was not legal. I will say that it was an outrage.

A&G: What was it like playing in Canada from 1959–1966?

Kapp: Geographically, they're next to this big country, the United States of America. And they didn't have the same number of leagues and players, but the Dominion of Canada is filled with wonderful people.

A&G: With your stats and influence playing football as well as coaching football, why are you not in the Pro Football Hall of Fame?

Kapp: Let me just say this. I took NFL to court when the Vikings let me go, and the Boston Patriots had me under contract, and would not let me play the 1971 season. I won a summary judgment in 1976. San Francisco's 9th circuit Court of Appeals said we're not going to tell you how to run the NFL, but this man's trade has been restrained. So what was the result of that? It was a legal point that the NFL had to give something away: the option clause. So players won free agency.

I am told that in sports law, my case is put up as the classic case of anti-trust. Was I damaged? Well, I never played football again after that.

A&G: There was some controversy when you were signed with the Patriots, but when you showed up you were turned away for practice and Jim Plunkett was brought on. Was it a case of there not being enough room on the field for two Latinos?

Kapp: During my time in Boston they offered me almost anything I wanted, but only if I would sign a standard player contract that would've

DOI: 10.1057/9781137403094

waived all my rights. The head of the players' union, said, "No, you have a contract. There's no such thing as a standard player contract." This was 1969. When I showed up to train, I was ordered out of the Patriots training camp, even though I had a contract to play for the 1970–1972 seasons. It took till 1976 to win in San Francisco court—but the vilification had already happened. Then commissioner of the NFL, Pete Rozelle, and the then Dolphins coach Don Shula—a cornerback I'd thrown seven touchdown passes against when he was a player—vilified me: Joe Kapp was not a good football player, he was only a good kickoff man. They absolutely lied.

I give credit to my Vikings teammate and fellow quarterback in 1969, Gary Cuozzo, for speaking out in favor of me. Others like John Brody and Jim Brown were nowhere to be found. Nobody supported me, but the law did. I armed myself with being correct in the law and on the field. All I ever wanted was to have a great football and coaching career in the U.S. Sometimes you get it and sometimes you don't.

A&G: You began your college and pro career as a football player over 50 years ago when you were the only Latino out there. In 1970 you appeared on the cover of *Sports Illustrated* announced as "The Toughest Chicano"...

Kapp: The only time my teammates cared that I was Latino was when I'd get my care packages in Minnesota and Canada from my mother. She would send chili and tortillas—and suddenly everybody was my pal. You have to imagine, this was back when there wasn't a taco stand to be seen from California to Vancouver, Calgary, Saskatchewan, Ontario. This was a time when nobody cared about Latinos. There were Latino players identifiable by their names like Chi Chi Rodríguez and Lee Trevino, but Latinos weren't even on the census back then. As a Latino football player I've experienced a lot of disappointments in my life, but I have always tried to stay positive.

A&G: This conversation is certainly just a snapshot of your life; a small nibble for our readers. You are writing a book on your life.

Kapp: It's a book I've been working on for some time now that tells the story not only of my life as a football player, but the whole of my journey in the world—as a son, brother, father, husband, grandfather, friend, and much much more...

* * *

DOI: 10.1057/9781137403094

Tom Flores

Frederick Luis Aldama & Christopher González: You were a young Latino who grew up in a family with modest means and that moved with the crop-picking seasons in rural California. It wouldn't seem from your early life experiences as a Latino that pro football would have been in the cards for you.

Tom Flores: It never did dawn on me that this was possible. I began first grade as a five-year-old in a grammar school that had eight grades and no kindergarten; while there was a mix of Latino, white kids and Asian kids, some didn't even have shoes. At school I remember trading bean and rice burritos my mom made fresh every morning for baloney sandwiches. It was a modest life. While we didn't have a TV, we did have a radio that my dad listened to. Outside of boxing and baseball, we had no Latino sports heroes.

A&G: So how did football enter into the picture?

Flores: My brother and I played lots of sports—all the kids played some sport or another outside. But it wasn't until we moved to Sanger, California, that my brother and I began to play other sports like basketball and football. They were simply a part of the school sports curriculum.

It just so happened I could throw well a ball or a football. And I enjoyed it. At that time, basketball was my favorite sport, with baseball coming in second, and football third. Thank God, somebody realized I was a little better at football than I was at the other two.

A&G: There's a long tradition of Latinos playing soccer and baseball, but not so much football. In the early days of football's pro leagues, there were Latinos but mostly as kickers...

Flores: Soccer's a Latin American game, so it's not surprising that these early Latinos in pro football were soccer kickers. You have to consider, too, that there weren't a lot of 200-plus pound Latinos running around. In my youth I had some Latino friends who were really good athletes, but they never got very big; they never went any further in football than high school. It was a rare moment when a Latino came around who was physically able to do what the pro leagues were looking for. I just happened to be one of those guys.

A&G: What was most remarkable about this early development of your sense of yourself as a football player—as an athlete generally?

DOI: 10.1057/9781137403094

Flores: The biggest competition I had growing up was with my older brother. I always hung around with him and his buddies who were all a couple of years older than me; because I started school so young, by the time my high school senior year rolled around I was a 16-year-old surrounded by a bunch of 18 years old. In other words, I developed as an athlete with guys that were older and bigger than me. If you're going to compete with older guys, you'd be better or as good. This certainly made me more competitive in a very quiet way.

A&G: With all the work that your parents had to do to put food on the table, there was likely not much time for someone like your dad to introduce the sport.

Flores: He would occasionally play some softball, but definitely not football. He didn't even know what basketball or football was until my brother and I started playing. There was nobody in the family that pointed us in any direction.

A&G: Many Latino families that have come from hardship tend to push us in directions where they think we are most likely to make a living like becoming an engineer or a doctor or…

Flores: My parents never pushed me in any one particular direction. They always supported everything that they did. There was an unspoken tradition in large Latino families that the oldest in the family would go to school to further their education while the rest of the kids would help support the family. Even though there was only me and my brother and I loved school, when I was growing up I never thought about going beyond high school. I always thought my brother would go because he was the oldest and very bright. As I went from junior into my senior year I realized that I wanted to continue with my education. The school I really wanted to go to was Stanford. I had the right grades, but not the right classes to get in so I went to junior college and then transferred to the four-year College of the Pacific.

A&G: Football in high school today has become very structured—with summer camps and the like we might even say that it has become professionalized.

Flores: In my day we never had the summer camps. We never had passing camps. We didn't have spring training for the football teams. It was also less specialized. At my small school I would play different sports like football, basketball, and baseball on different days of the week. We didn't

DOI: 10.1057/9781137403094

have technical summer camps, passing camps. We certainly didn't have weightlifting as part of our training. I went to school, played sports, and when this was done, I went to work in the fields—until I got my job in the ice plant—to save as much money as possible.

For kids today, sports is a year-round training that works in very specialized ways: football players train to play football, basketball players train to play basketball, and baseball players train to play baseball. And this all starts in junior high and earlier. This early training to improve their skills along with a greater awareness of diet today is growing bigger and faster athletes.

In my day you just evolved into a player by your own instincts. Nobody taught me how to throw a football. I picked up the football the very first day, and I threw a spiral and thought: wow, this is fun. Because I could throw the ball the best, I started playing quarterback.

A&G: Can you speak to some memorable experiences you might have had as a Latino football player while you were at either Fresno City College or the College of Pacific.

Flores: Growing up right after WWII in a valley town I was used to interacting with a mix of kids: white, Latino, and Asian—Japanese that had experienced the internment camps. This was normal. When I went away to college, this changed. Mostly I experienced being stereotyped when dating. Later when I went into the pro leagues, and traveled back East or the Midwest most people didn't even know what a Latino was.

When I was a kid, I was a Mexican, and then I became a Latino, and then I became a Chicano, and then I became a Hispanic. But like I used to tell a buddy, "I'm more American than you guys because us Latinos were here first." In many ways playing sports meant not having to deal with racism directly. I mean I never had the door slammed in my face. I never was called a name. I never went through some of the things some of the ethnic groups have gone through. I saw it. I didn't like it. But I was in never in a position where I could stand up and make a statement about racism. I wanted to fight those battles I knew I had a chance of winning.

A&G: Joe Kapp, you, and Jim Plunkett certainly broke open a bunch of seemingly locked doors: you as a player then as a coach. Your career has opened doors to other Latinos playing pro football.

DOI: 10.1057/9781137403094

Flores: I'll always proud of what I have been able to accomplish in my early education and college—both on the field and in the classroom as a student. But it never dawned on me until I went into the pro leagues and became the first Hispanic and Mexican quarterback in a brand new football league that it became larger than me. My presence in pro football touched a chord nationally. This continued after I became the first Latino head coach and then took the Raiders to win a Super Bowl. I especially felt the significance of being the first Latino at all these levels when I traveled through the densely Latino populated Southwest—and of course, when I traveled to Mexico. The people let me know how proud they were of my accomplishments as a Latino.

But my mind was on other things. By my second year as a head coach for the Raiders I had resurrected Jim Plunkett who became our quarterback. Papers were filled with speculations about getting fired after the fourth or fifth game because we were two and three. My boss, Al Davis, was not very happy. And I said, "Listen!" I said, "Al, we're not doing anything wrong. We have to do it better. And we will." We jelled as a team and we did get better after the fifth game, going and winning the Super Bowl. The elation and the exuberance of winning and being champions and succeeding in one of the toughest businesses there is in professional sports, and doing it the way we did, it was overwhelming. I was just doing the best job I could. I was working hard to open doors, closing those behind me when I failed. It wasn't till after the fact that I could look back and take pride in what I had been able to accomplish as a Latino in the pro leagues.

It wasn't until later in life after most of this was over that I realized how proud I made my family and many, many other Latinos across the country: "He's a Mexicano." Of course, my mother would remind me not to get too big for my britches...and "don't you spit on television, or scratch"—the typical Mexican mom who brings us down to earth.

A&G: We are seeing more Latino kids in high school today that are bigger, faster, and better trained but we still don't see as many Latino players or coaches in the NFL as we might expect. We've got the Mark Sanchezes, Tony Gonzálezes, and Tony Romos, but we should have many more.

Flores: Back when I was playing it was a real oddity for a Latino player to come along; we just weren't physically built to be big. When someone like the giant of a football player Anthony Muñoz came along it was a rare exception. I told him: "You're the biggest Hispanic I've ever seen in my life." There just weren't a lot of Anthony Muñozes walking around in the barrios. Where I live now in the Palm Springs area, we have a lot of Latinos playing football in high school and many go on to play pretty well in college. Some choose not to play sports in college, though. My twin boys were great athletes and great at math, they both chose careers that had to do with numbers and not sports.

A&G: The doors that have opened might be more than just in the athletic world. We are both professors and our parents were not, for instance. Yet, there does seem to be a precipitous drop from all the Latino football players in high school to the few in the pro football leagues. It looks like the NFL is just not that interested in recruiting Latinos.

Flores: Right now there is a mandate in the National Football League that if there is a coaching position open, you have to interview at least one "minority" coach. But they have a specific minority in mind—a black minority.

When I was in Seattle as the president and general manager, we had a minority-coaching program. Bill Walsh started it with the 49ers when he brought in a college coach, and they were always black. And I said, "Well, why does it have to be black? It's a minority program, so let's include and train all minorities, Hispanics included." We did bring in a black coach from college to work through the summer training camp with us but we also brought in a Latino, Juan Castillo. Both continued training in the following year then were hired. To my knowledge, I was the first guy to ever do that in the NFL.

A&G: The NFL is certainly more racially and ethnically diverse today than in your days of coaching.

Flores: Today, 80 percent of the players in the NFL are black, but we need to have more blacks that can do a great job in management and in PR. Mike Taylor is with the Raiders because he does a great job. When we have more Latinos in the locker room, we'll need more Latinos in management and PR.

A&G: Looking in from the outside there's still that sense that no matter how talented a Latino player is, he might not get a shot at the NFL because of prejudice.

Flores: Talent surfaces. Look at Jim Plunkett. When he was at Stanford they wanted to move him to linebacker because they thought he lacked

DOI: 10.1057/9781137403094

the finesse needed to quarterback. He was stood his ground and eventually won the Heisman Trophy as a quarterback. The talent surfaced.

A&G: The city of Oakland first named the Oakland Raiders the "Oakland Señors." Oakland today is a very densely populated Latino city. And earlier you mentioned your travels through the Southwest. Can you talk about your experience with fans and the communities they represent?

Flores: The way we played in those days they should have called us the Oakland Señoritas. In any case, it's a good thing the Oakland Señors didn't stick as the name for the new, Oakland-based AFL franchise. Today, the Raiders have become a great symbol as well as *the* team of the Hispanics. Wherever you travel you'll find many, many Latino fans dressed in their silver and black. San Diego probably has the biggest Raider booster club in any city, even bigger than the one in Oakland, and they're almost all Latinos.

A&G: Fans can be your best friend—and your worst enemy. Mark Sanchez made the cover of all sorts of magazines as a superstar but after he makes mistakes on the field, he falls quickly from grace.

Flores: Unfortunately Mark's playing in the toughest city in the world: New York City. They can make you king, or they can make you the worst person in the world overnight. Fans can be cruel. I know that from the experience of playing in different cities—some were worse than others. I never received too many ethnic slurs, but I certainly received my share of expletives playing in cities like Denver—one of the worst. And, I got my share of hate mail—some of it came from prejudice but never of any consequence. And in 1960–1961 when we traveled through the South I experienced prejudice along with our black players when we were refused service in a hotel—they must have forgotten that they lost the Civil War. Their prejudice was directed at the black players, and not Latinos. But you have to remember that they didn't have any prejudice toward Latino players because they probably didn't even know what that was in those days.

A&G: As one of the first Latino players and coaches out of the gate, you've seen the game evolve over a long period of time and from the frontlines.

Flores: It's changed for better and worse. First, the game has gotten bigger than life. This isn't so surprising. As television grew in popularity, so too has the game. It's a sport that is perfectly suited for television:

DOI: 10.1057/9781137403094

slow-mo, instant replay, all that stuff is perfect for football. There is no other sport so well matched for TV. Soccer is too spread out and continuous in its movement. Baseball is too slow. Basketball is too fast. With football you run a play that takes about 7 to 10 seconds with about 30 seconds in between to show the slow motion replay while talking about it.

The large sums of money have changed the attitudes of the players. This isn't bad. Players deserve what they get, but it has changed a few of them. Many of these guys are good to their families and support all sorts of important charities. Unfortunately, the media are less interested in the good achieved by many of the players. The negative tabloid stories that run on football are one of the changes for the worse. Blogs are more interested in following who was arrested. So the players have to be smarter than the media.

A&G: You've encountered several crossroads in your life, and clearly you've made all the right choices in terms of your career and so on. If you looked back over your career might there have been a moment when you thought that should have done this differently.

Flores: I would have maybe trained a little differently to get myself into better shape. If I had been in better shape, my career might have lasted longer. In today's marketplace I could have played another five years. That said, I was ten years in the game—a lot longer than the average person. The average person is still 3½, 4 years. We just didn't have the same opportunities that players have today with off-season training. I would have also chosen to major in the medical field. Probably, if I had done this I would not have gone into the pro leagues. So in a way I'm glad I didn't.

A&G: It could have been very different for you.

Flores: Yes, like my older brother who was a great athlete. He and the head coach did not get along, so he quit the team his senior year in high school. And, even though he was an A student, he decided to quit school as well. He went to work, got married, and had a baby right away. Later he went into business for himself with a restaurant and bar. But he always kept thinking that because he didn't go to college that he was a failure. I think down deep he wishes that he could have been me.

*   *   *

DOI: 10.1057/9781137403094

Jim Plunkett

Frederick Luis Aldama & Christopher González: Let's start with some of questions about your early days growing up as a Latino kid first in Santa Clara then San Jose. This seems to be a time when there weren't any Latinos playing football.

Plunkett: When we moved from Santa Clara to San Jose and then farther to the east side of San Jose, most of us who played sports in the streets and on schoolyards were Hispanic. Because most of those who live on the east side were Hispanic, most of the guys I played with were Hispanic; there were also a few black, Asian, and white kids. We all played sports like football, basketball, baseball, you name it—and most of us were Hispanic. When I went on to play football in high school at James Lick, while there was quite a mixture of ethnicities and races many of the team members were also Hispanic.

A&G: Your high school football coach, Al Cementina, was an important role model and mentor, showing you that you could become a football player. Can you speak to this as well as other influences and experiences that opened your eyes to the possibility that you could actually be a pro football player?

Plunkett: In high school and before, I didn't think about becoming a professional player. I was just excited to be on a football team. But I also played baseball, basketball, and wrestled—along with a lot of other sports. However, by the time I got to be a junior in high school, I knew that football was the direction I wanted to go with. My love for the game of football transcended all these other sports. I was also very competitive. I like to be better than the guy next to me or in front of me. If some guy was better than me at something, I worked hard enough to try to get better than him. I liked to win.

Al Cementina was very clear sighted about my academic and athletic abilities, knowing where I could go to college. I had good enough grades and I was a perfect quarterback for the team—a small team with a lot of Hispanics. I knew how to throw the football, spread it around the field, get it to guys who can make plays and run with the ball after the catch. I loved playing for Cementina—a coach who could get the most out of his athletes. We only lost one game in two years—a testament to Cementina's coaching and to my teammates who refused to get beaten down by the

DOI: 10.1057/9781137403094

bigger guys. They offered me the protection I needed to get the job done as a quarterback. I'm very proud of those tough, hard-nosed, scrappy Mexicans. Back in those days we went by Mexican and not Hispanic....

A&G: The odds were stacked against you—especially as an up-and-coming athlete. With your parents blind you helped take care of the family; you needed to wear glasses, and suffered from knee problems... This hardly fits the profile of the gifted athlete you became.

Plunkett: I suffered from Osgood-Schlatter disease. Kids who grow quickly tend to suffer from this. The soft tissue doesn't grow as quickly as your bone structure, causing problems—and pain—with your knees. In the 7th grade I had to stop playing football and basketball. The doctor wanted me to stop playing for a year. I couldn't do it, so I had went out for baseball at the end of the year. The pain was sometimes hard to deal with, but I got through it.

A&G: You started working to help the family out at a pretty young age.

Plunkett: You know, I picked fruit in the summers. After school I worked at a gas station cleaning up for two hours before they closed, making a couple bucks an hour—whatever it was back then. I went home for dinner and tried to study to get ready for school the next day.

A&G: Your academic and athletic diligence and hard work paid off. You made it to Stanford.

Plunkett: Before I was out the door to go to Stanford, I thought my career was over. They discovered a tumor on my thyroid. I called up one of the recruiting coaches, Rod Rusk, to let him know that I might not be able to play for Stanford. His response: "We want you to come to Stanford anyway, whether you play football for us or not." This endeared me to Stanford. During this era, if you couldn't play football other universities would have withdrawn the scholarship.

A&G: Can you tell us about your experiences at Stanford as a Latino.

Plunkett: It was tough for me. I had no money. My parents didn't have some of the basics that other kids had like a car, for instance. I felt a little embarrassed and out of place. On top of this, football wasn't going well for me. I did have surgery and it slowed my progress down on the football field. During my first two years I was not doing well at football. This increased my sense of not fitting in and not doing well in my classes. I thought about leaving. On the team, they considered changing

DOI: 10.1057/9781137403094

my position from quarterback to defensive end. That made me even less happy. It was a real struggle for me those first couple years.

A&G: If you could point to something that helped turn this struggle, what would it be?

Plunkett: Getting healthy again, playing and throwing the football the way I did before I got hurt and had surgery to remove the tumor. The surgery really set me back. When football started going well, my classes started going better. I felt more comfortable at school.

My football teammates played an important part in this turn. I met a lot of them before going to Stanford because of recruiting trips to other schools around the country. We were all struggling a little bit, so we leaned on one another's shoulder to make it through. It's not easy. In high school, you're a big fish in a little pond. You get to a big university; you wind up being a small fish in a huge, huge ocean, and trying to fit in, trying to make things right. It was a very difficult period, but I didn't want to give up.

A&G: You went from Stanford into the NFL, making history. Some others didn't make the draft and had to cross the border into the Canadian Football League then come back to the NFL. This seemed to be the case for a lot of the Latino players.

Plunkett: I never realized this. Maybe other "non-Latino" players also went up there to play before coming back here. I don't know the ratio of Latino vs. non-Latino players that did this so I can't make a comment on it, other than the fact that it gave them a chance to improve their skills, get better, and then find a place in the NFL.

A&G: When you made history by taking the Raiders to two Super Bowl victories (1981 and 1984) there were only a few Latinos in the leagues. Today, we see much more diversity. This is likely to do with the size of Latinos generally as well as opportunities to play and train as football players.

Plunkett: There is no doubt that the NFL is much more diverse today. Growing up in the '50s and '60s I was a big guy for a Hispanic. Fortunately, for me, I had this growth spurt when I went from a short, fat kid to a tall, thin kid just at the right time. But my starting right guard was tough as nails, but he was only 135 pounds so his football future was literally nil. He just wasn't big enough to play.

DOI: 10.1057/9781137403094

And, yes, today they have all these football camps at universities or private camps that you can go to improve your skills. You can go to guys who can make you stronger, faster, and improve your ability to play. We didn't have that in our day. We learned our football in the streets. We played basketball in the court outside. And as far as baseball was concerned, the Ford was first base, the Chevy across the street second base.

A&G: Playing for the Raiders appears to have brought together all right ingredients for you to bring the team to two Super Bowl victories.

Plunkett: First, you don't win without players, and we had a lot of great players like wide receiver Fred Biletnikoff, guard Gene Upshaw, and defensive back Ted Watts. The players we had were great analysts of the game. It was a perfect fit for me. Playing with these guys allowed me to do what I do best: throw the football with the goal of leading the team to victory. We had a lot of nutty players, but when it came time to play and suit up on Sunday, they were ready to go get the job done. Their singular focus: to win football games. Al Davis helped create this atmosphere. He didn't care what baggage you had dragging along behind you, as long as you played for him on Sundays. The atmosphere of this period with the Raiders was tremendous.

A&G: With your stats and influence we wonder why you're not in the Pro Football Hall of Fame.

Plunkett: While my numbers aren't the best, there are certainly a few players in the Hall of Fame with worse stats. Namath is there with one Super Bowl victory. I won two. Tom [Flores] should be in it and other non-Hispanic players like wide receiver Cliff Branch who won three Super Bowl rings playing with the Raiders. For whatever reason, we've been overlooked.

A&G: You and Tom have the Raiders in common but also you both come from humble Latino roots.

Plunkett: Tom and I hit it off. We do have a similar background. He knew what I was going through when I joined the team. He shared his experiences with me, helping me prepare better for each and every football game and to become a better quarterback.

A&G: The Latino fan base is huge today.

Plunkett: Number one, Hispanics love football—teams and individual players. I had a large following in the Hispanic community. I connected

DOI: 10.1057/9781137403094

with the fact that I was born and raised in the Santa Clara Valley yet was able to make it. I like to think that Tom and I and others do give some hope. A lot of Hispanics are still struggling in this country, so to actually see what you can accomplish if you set your mind to it can be inspiring. I didn't set out to be a professional football player or baseball player or any other sport. We were on welfare. We were poor. We lived in crummy houses. My parents weren't very educated. I ended up going to Stanford then playing pro football. This kind of story gives people hope.

When I was growing up I didn't have any Hispanic role models to look up to. I listened to a lot of the baseball games on the radio, becoming a fan of the Yankees because of Mickey Mantle and Roger Maris. Quarterbacks like Johnny Unitas and Bart Starr performing on the football field made an impression. I thought that if I could combine their talents then I'd be on my way to being a pretty good quarterback.

A&G: Certainly, the media back when you were growing up was not what it is today, but had you heard of Joe Kapp—another history-making Latino football player?

Plunkett: Like my non-Hispanic sounding last name, Kapp's also fooled people. So I really didn't know he was Hispanic until I was maybe 25 or 26. He wasn't visible as a figure for me to look up to when I was younger.

A&G: Is there anything you would have done differently, looking back at your career?

Plunkett: I did what I had to do at the time. I worked hard. I practiced. I wanted to be a better player after practice than I was before practice. I tried to become a better player every time I stepped on the field. I didn't like to lose. I was always competitive. But there was something else driving me. Since I was a little kid I wanted to make a better life for my family and me as I grew up.

DOI: 10.1057/9781137403094

Epilogue: End Zones and New Scrimmage Lines

Abstract: *"End Zones and New Scrimmage Lines,"* reminds readers of the history covered in the book: from deep cultural history (the Mesoamerican game of ulama) that began the book to discussions of the brown color line, to the rise and fall of Latino superstar players. The Epilogue reminds readers of the significant role Latinos have played in the shaping of the NFL.

Frederick Luis Aldama and Christopher González. *Latinos in the End Zone: Conversations on the Brown Color Line in the NFL.* New York: Palgrave Macmillan, 2014.
DOI: 10.1057/9781137403094.

DOI: 10.1057/9781137403094

Frederick Luis Aldama: In our *conversación de sobremesa* we've covered a lot of turf, Christopher: From deep cultural history (the Mesoamerican, *ulama*) to education to trends in regional habitation to brown color lines in and off the field to the role of the community, the media, and capitalism generally in the rise and fall of Latino superstar players.

Christopher González: As the life stories of Kapp, Flores, and Plunkett so insightfully reveal, there is a rich history of Latinos giving shape to what has become *the* cultural centerpiece of everyday life in the U.S.

FLA: As we look back on our recovery work we might reflect a moment on the solidification of what appears to be a paradox. In this *conversación de sobremesa* we make visible the presence of Latinos in the history of the NFL—a presence that today is becoming more and more filled out with Latino players that are making normal (naturalizing, say) their presence. When Romo appears with Jessica Simpson in *People* magazine, it's not as a *Latino* per se; it's not to announce his Latinidad. It's as a good-ole boy who quarterbacks for the Cowboys. Might our making visible the moment of our arrival in the NFL also mark the moment of our erasure in the NFL—and sports generally...

Christopher González: Yes, and no. Historically, Latinos have been invisible in the NFL because—for a variety of reasons—they weren't *in* the NFL in large numbers, but they were there in *significant* areas such as Kapp, Flores, and Plunkett. So the work of recovering or making visible this overlooked history is crucial, work we've done here and work others will continue. As Latinos become more and more a significant aspect of the NFL, our presence will be recognized, and hopefully, appreciated. Yet I see what you're saying, that an ideal situation is one in which Latinos appear in the NFL while few give it a second thought because it is so expected. But in order to get to that point, we need to acknowledge our history in the NFL as well as the significant moments along the way, as we've done here.

FLA: Another way we might spin this is to put a finger on that anxious pulse that beats around the sense that while American football is, as you point out, watched more and more by Latinos it is at the same time becoming culturally dominant. The anxiety spelled out in so many words: we arrive as players and spectators (televisual or otherwise) at the moment of sweeping to the side of Latino mainstays such as boxing, baseball, soccer, rodeos (*charrería*), and the *lucha libre*.

DOI: 10.1057/9781137403094

CG: Those sports that are Latino mainstays may never rise to the level of popularity as American football, but that doesn't mean they are going away anytime soon. To stake a claim now in the dominant sport in America is a moment of significance that cannot be underestimated. What it speaks to is that Latinos—with the right circumstances and resources—can compete in all sorts of professional sports. In so many respects, sports are used as a marker of humanity. Recall those minority players who were not allowed to play professional sports. Remember the stereotypes that even persist to this day that claim certain marginalized groups are incapable of playing one type of sport or another. A way to mark someone as "other" or not equal is to keep him or her from playing professional sports. To dispel with those exclusionist policies and stereotypes is a healthy thing for American sports.

FLA: Yes, Latinos have faced this athletic exclusionism in all sports. Today, with their own stories of struggle respective to each sport, we seem to be appearing more and more across the full range of sports. We're competing in water and on dirt as well as on ice and well manicured turfs and other traditionally non-Latino identified spaces. Does the presence of Latinos such as Lee Trevino, Juan "Chi Chi" Rodriguez, Nancy Lopez, Lorena Ochoa, Lizette Salas in the world of golf mean that *we've arrived*? Does having Scott Gomez and Bill Guerin in pro hockey, Dara Torres setting U.S. swimming records, and pro BMX-ers like Mike "Rooftop" Escamilla mean that *we've arrived*? Does having a laundry list of Latinos playing basketball such as Alfred "Butch" Lee, Rocky Galarza, Mark Aguirre, Rolando Blackman, Eduardo Nájera, Paul Gasol, Carmelo Anthony, Carlos Arroyo, and Emmanuel "Manu" Ginobili, Leandro Barbosa, and Al Horford mean *we've arrived*?

CG: I hesitate to use the phrase *we've arrived* because it suggests stasis or finality to me. It indicates that we're here, and now everything that kept us out is no long a factor. Perhaps we should say *we're capable* instead. The success of these Latinos in other sports is an indication that *we're capable* of playing at the most elite level. To say *we've arrived* again makes me think of the election of President Obama. For many it signaled some sort of "post-racial" moment in the U.S.; that an African American president of the United States suddenly meant African Americans *had arrived*, and that all of the institutionalized barriers faced by that community were suddenly null and void. Jackie Robinson's inclusion in professional baseball wasn't the end. It was the beginning. He was proof that African

DOI: 10.1057/9781137403094

Americans were just as capable of playing at that elite level of baseball as white players.

FLA: Yes, I like *we're capable* much better, Christopher. Let me turn briefly to another thorny issue that has come up in our *conversación*: the deep contradictions present in sports that exist within the socioeconomic system of capitalism. Detroit just filed for bankruptcy—it's for sale to the highest bidder. Yet at the same time, it's able to pull together the public funding to finish building its multimillion-dollar professional ice hockey arena.

I mention this to bring us back to the elephant in the room we've been pointing at in our *conversación* about Latino athletes in pro sports generally. Is all this simply a way to divert our attention from the issues at stake: the issue of increasing socioeconomic inequality rooted in deep problems concerning equal access to the full resources of education that would allow Latinos (and all others) the possibility of realizing their total potentialities. This could be as the next Plunkett or the next Einstein or both in the same person.

CG: I can hardly believe a major American city as Detroit can be in such disrepair. Here in Texas we've come to expect high school to build football stadiums that are more appropriate for mid-size universities. Imagine a high school that uses decades-old textbooks with little to no technology in the classroom suddenly building a multi-million dollar football stadium. It defies common sense and decency. I'm not against state of the art facilities, but where are our priorities?

FLA: I think this points us back to education, Christopher. The story of Latinos in the NFL also seems to highlight a more general concern: where will the twisted and often contradictory tracks lead this train when on the one hand physical education programs are being wiped out in many regions at the lower education levels yet spending on athletic programs like football at the university level seem to be on the rise. Where's this train going to end up when these two contradictory movements are intensified by a public education system that's pulled the plug on academic investment at all the educational levels.

CG: To me it indicates a return to the elitism of early football when only the sons of America's upper crust could enter these programs. With high schools featuring multi-million dollar football stadiums and top-of-the-line training and playing equipment, how can small, rural programs

DOI: 10.1057/9781137403094

produce players who can compete for those few spots in programs like Alabama, Ohio State, Texas, Michigan, and USC? High schools are becoming mini-versions of the top collegiate football programs. All the while, the educational aspects of these public schools are being trimmed, pruned, and hacked beyond recognition.

FLA: As our *conversación de sobremesa* has shown, we know that for better or worse (generally worse) there's no denying that we exist within a capitalist socioeconomic system. Throwing up the hands won't change this. Perhaps, however, we can make a difference—not just in telling this story, but also as teachers and, as you point out earlier in the book, as role models.

CG: Yes. Teachers and role models are *crucial* to how the system can get out of this spiral. The problem is that it sounds like such a cliché. But in reality, nothing changes a student nor gives him or her hope like a mentor or role model, and specifically role models that look like they come from the same kind of neighborhood as the student. Additionally, teachers shouldn't shoulder the entire burden. As a former high school English teacher, I can tell you that a teacher's life is stressful and exhausting. When people grouse at how teachers only work for nine months a year, they fail to consider that teachers work all day at school and then come home to continue to work by grading, lesson planning, and so on, as well as on weekends and holidays. Thus, we need more role models that come from all walks of the professional community. Adults need to begin to volunteer time at their local schools. For a few years now I've argued that all school districts should require every parent or guardian of a child enrolled in its schools to devote two days per school year as an all-day volunteer. Not only would it benefit the students, it would increase the level of investment on the part of parents. Whatever we do, we're going to need to roll up our sleeves. That's a given.

FLA: Vargas Llosa considered our experience of sports as short-lived entertainment—as a spectacle. Unlike a novel or play, sports for Vargas Llosa do "not transcend the physical, the sensory, the instant emotion." Sports "scarcely leaves a trace in the memory and does not enrich or impoverish knowledge." I wonder, however, if *Latinos in the End Zone* might in fact enrich our knowledge of sports and stretch wide our perception, thought, and feeling about football—and sports generally.

DOI: 10.1057/9781137403094

CG: I have to disagree with Vargas Llosa; sports *do* transcend the physical, the sensory—the instant emotion! It leaves much more than a trace in the memory, and it certainly can enrich knowledge. So many lessons that have shaped me as a person came from my own participation in sports. I can remember so many times watching sports with my brothers and my father that I can tell you exactly where I was when I watched certain games or events, and I cherish those memories. What's more, sports can give kids something around which to shape their identity and a reason to push themselves in school and pursue higher education.

Our discussion regarding Latinos in the NFL suddenly makes visible the Latino presence in the most dominant of American sports. It has certainly allowed me to have a new understanding of just how important Latinos have been and will continue to be as consumers and shapers of American sports and American culture.

FLA: I hear you loud and clear, Christopher. Let's continue to do our work in and out of the classroom to open more doors for the next generation of Latinos to realize their dreams—as football players and all else imaginable and even unimaginable...

DOI: 10.1057/9781137403094

Works Cited and Suggested Reading

Acosta, Oscar "Zeta". "From Whence I Came," in *Oscar "Zeta" Acosta: The Uncollected Works*. Houston: Arte Público Press, 1996.

Alamillo, José M. "Playing Across Borders: Transnational Sports and Identities in Southern California and Mexico, 1930–1945," *Pacific Historical Review* 79, no. 3 (2010): 360–392.

Alvarez, Barry with Mike Lucas. *Don't Flinch: Barry Alvarez: The Autobiography*. Champaign, IL: KCI Sports, 2006.

Amador de Gama, Luis. Ed. *Historia Gráfica del fútbol americano en México, I: 1936–1945*. México DF: Olmeca Impresiones Finas, 1982.

Arbena, Joseph L. "The Later Evolution of Modern Sport in Latin America: The North American Influence," *The International Journal of the History of Sport* 18, no. 3 (September 2001): 43–58.

Burgos, Adrian Jr. *Playing America's Game: Baseball, Latinos, and the Color Line*. Berkeley: University of California Press, 2007.

Carlos Kevin Blanton. "From Intellectual Deficiency to Cultural Deficiency: Mexican Americans, Test and Public School Policy in the American Southwest, 1920–1940," *Pacific Historical Review* 72 (2003): 39–62.

Cashion, Ty. *Pigskin Pulpit: A Social History of Texas High School Football Coaches*. Austin: Texas State Historical Association, 1998.

Corpí, Lucha. *Black Widow's Wardrobe*. Houston: Arte Público Press, 1999.

DOI: 10.1057/9781137403094

DeLillo, Don. *End Zone*. Boston: Houghton Mifflin, 1972.

Faflik, David. "Fútbol America: Hemispheric Sport as Border Studies," *Americana* 5, no. 1 (2006): 1–12.

Flores, Tom with Bob O'Connor. *Coaching Football*. New York: McGraw-Hill, 1998.

Flores, Tom with Frank Cooney. *Fire in the Iceman: Autobiography of Tom Flores*. Los Angeles: Bonus Books, 1992.

Flores, Tom with Matt Fulks. *Tales from the Oakland Raiders*. Champaign, IL: Sports Publishing, LLC, 2007.

Gems, Gerald. *The Athletic Crusade: Sport and American Cultural Imperialism*. Lincoln: University of Nebraska Press, 2006.

Hogan, Patrick Colm. *Understanding Nationalism: On Narrative, Cognitive Science, and Identity*. Columbus: The Ohio State University Press, 2009.

———. *What Literature Teaches Us about Emotion*. Cambridge: Cambridge University Press, 2011.

Iber, Jorge and Samuel O. Regalado, *Mexican Americans and Sports: A Reader on Athletics and Barrio Life*. Lubbock, TX: Texas A & M University Press, 2007.

Iber, Jorge, Samuel Regaldo, Jose Alamillo, and Arnoldo De Leon. *Latinos in U.S. Sport: A History of Isolation, Cultural Identity, and Acceptance*. Champaign, IL: Human Kinetics, 2011.

Izenberg, Jerry. *Great Latin Sports Figures*. New York, NY: Doubleday & Company Inc., 1976.

Jamieson, Katherine M. "Reading Nancy Lopez: Decoding Representations of Race, Gender and Sexuality," *Sociology of Sport Journal* 15, no. 4 (1998): 343–358.

Lomax, Michael E. Ed. *Sports and the Racial Divide: African American and Latino Experience in an Era of Change*. Jackson: University Press of Mississippi, 2008.

Longoria, Mario. *Athletes Remembered: Mexicano/Latino Professional Football Players 1929-1970* Tempe: Bilingual Review Press, 1997.

Maltby, Marc. S. *The Origins and Early Development of Professional Football*. New York: Garland Publishing, Inc., 1997.

Marín, Marely. "Futbol American Femenil," in *Yarda 50: La Revista del Futbol Americano de México* 1999 .

Messner, M. "When Bodies Are Weapons: Masculinity and Violence in Sport," *International Review for the Sociology of Sport* vol. 25 (September 1990): 203–215.

DOI: 10.1057/9781137403094

Mitchell, Elmer. "Racial Traits in Athletics," *American Physical Education Review* 27, no. 4 (April 1922): 147–152.

Plunkett, Jim with Dave Newhouse. *The Jim Plunkett Story: The Saga of a Man Who Came Back*. Westminster, MD: Arbor House Publications Co., 1981.

Prieto, Jorge. *The Quarterback Who Almost Wasn't*. Houston: Arte Público Press, 1994.

Ramos, Manuel. *The Ballad of Rocky Ruiz*. New York: St. Martin's Press, 1993.

Ross, Murray. "Football Red and Baseball Green: The Heroics and Bucolics of American Sport," *Chicago Review* vol. 22 (1971): 30–40.

Rowe, David, Jim McKay, and Toby Miller. "Panic Sport and the Racialized Masculine Body." In *Masculinities, Gender Relations, and Sport*. Eds. Jim McKay, Michael A. Messner, and Don Sabo. London: Sage Publications, 2000: 245–262.

Salas, Floyd. *Buffalo Nickel: A Memoir*. Houston: Arte Público Press, 1992.

Stavans, Ilan and Frederick Luis Aldama. *¡Muy Pop! Conversations on Latino Popular Culture*. Ann Arbor: University of Michigan Press, 2013.

Van Bottenburg, Maarten. *Global Games*. Urbana: University of Illinois Press, 2001.

Vargas Llosa, Mario. *Making Waves*. Ed. John King, FS & G, 1996.

Véa, Alfredo. *La Maravilla*. New York: Dutton, 1993.

Villarreal, José Antonio. *Clemente Chacon: A Novel*. Binghamton, NY: Bilingual Press, 1984.

DOI: 10.1057/9781137403094

Index

DOI: 10.1057/9781137403094

DOI: 10.1057/9781137403094

DOI: 10.1057/9781137403094

DOI: 10.1057/9781137403094

DOI: 10.1057/9781137403094

DOI: 10.1057/9781137403094